SHARE GUIDE
ASSOCIATION
(MALAYSIA)

With Compliments And Appreciation
From
The Share/Guide Association of Malaysia
1999

AMC - Melewar Zecha
Communications Sdn Bhd

•

Bank Bumiputra Malaysia Bhd

•

Bukit Young Goldmine Sdn Bhd

•

Esso Production Malaysia Inc.

•

GEC - Marconi

•

Globe Silk Store

•

Golden Hope Plantations Bhd

•

IGB Corporation Bhd

•

Kuching Hilton

•

Magnum Corporation Bhd

•

Malaysia LNG Sdn Bhd

•

Malaysia Mining Corporation
Bhd

•

Malaysia National Insurance
Sdn Bhd

•

Resorts World Bhd

•

Sapura Holding Sdn Bhd

•

Sime Darby Bhd

•

The Lion Group

•

The New Straits Times
Press (M) Bhd

•

DHL Sdn Bhd

•

Far East Offset &
Engraving Sdn Bhd

•

Sarawak State Government
Ministry of
Environment and Tourism

Pierre Argo

EDITORIAL ADVISORY BOARD

TAN SRI ZAIN AZRAAI BIN ZAINAL ABIDIN
Secretary-General of the Ministry of Finance

TAN SRI DATO' ABDUL AZIZ BIN ABDUL RAHMAN
Managing Director of Malaysia Airlines

TAN SRI THONG YAW HONG
Chairman of Sports Toto Malaysia Berhad

TAN SIR T.J. KISHU
Chairman of Globe Silk Store

DATO' ABDUL AZIZ BIN ISMAIL
Principal Private Secretary to the Prime Minister

ISMAIL ZAIN
Managing Director of Centre Stage

ISMAIL ADAM
Deputy Secretary-General
of the Ministry of Culture, Arts & Tourism

AZAH AZIZ
Writer

IBRAHIM HUSSEIN
Artist

•

PUBLISHER
Didier Millet

PROJECT DIRECTOR
Marina Mahathir Roussille

ASSOCIATE PROJECT DIRECTOR
Yvan van Outrive

PROJECT EDITOR
Peter Schoppert

CHIEF PHOTOGRAPHER
Luca Invernizzi Tettoni

EDITOR
Mary Lee

PROJECT CONSULTANTS
John Owen
Austen Zecha
Jim Holloway

•

CHIEF PROJECT COORDINATOR: Belinda Davies
Travel & Logistics Coordinator: Irene Tan
Kuala Lumpur Events Coordinator: June Baharuddin
Accounts: Louise Wong • *French Edition:* Jean-Pascal Elbaz
Public Relations Coordinator: Karen Roberts & Edelman Public Relations

ASSIGNMENT COORDINATORS
June Yunos • Chris Lee • Khoo Su Nin
Jim Holloway • Caroline Goh

PHOTO EDITORS
Marie-Claude Millet • Janie Joseland Bennett
Peter Schoppert • Luca Invernizzi Tettoni

DESIGN
Patrick Lebedeff • Louise Brody

PRODUCTION MANAGER
Edmund Lam

•

PROJECT ACCOUNTANTS: Price Waterhouse

MARKETING CONSULTANTS: Charles Kang & Ian Pringle

ADVERTISING AGENCY: AMC-Melewar Zecha Communications

•

MALAYSIA

HEART OF SOUTHEAST ASIA

PHOTOGRAPHS BY

46 OF THE WORLD'S

FINEST PHOTOGRAPHERS

WITH A FOREWORD BY

ADIBAH AMIN

AND ESSAYS BY

GAVIN YOUNG

AND

PAUL WACHTEL

•

AND CONTRIBUTIONS BY

LAT

JOHN FALCONER

MICHAEL FREEMAN

KHOO SU NIN

HEIDI MUNAN

SHOBA DEVAN

ARCHIPELAGO
PRESS

An ancient Malaysian tale tells of a spirit-princess of the mountains, who hid her heart so well that no suitor could capture it. Then a young village weaver, pining for her, guessed her secret. He asked his friends — creatures of the land, the water and the air — to bring him items from their domains which satisfied the strictest standards of truth and beauty. The finest of these he wove together and, sure enough, it was the heart of his beloved, the spirit-princess of the mountains. Malaysia, like the princess in this story of long ago, has evaded many an ardent attempt to capture her heart. And like the young suitor, the creators of this book have woven that elusive heart out of the finest items produced by forty-six sensitive and seasoned photographers, reinforced by illuminating words. For those of us Malaysians who feel we know this many-splendoured land, no selection could tally exactly with our individual notions of her 'heart'. We are sure to bemoan the absence of items which for us have always meant Malaysia; or to protest the inclusion of objects or views which do not seem central to this country. For the most part, however, we will welcome this book as an honest yet dramatic portrayal of Malaysia, in which diverse and contrasting parts form a living entity. It is interesting that the works of the five Malaysian photographers cannot easily be distinguished from those of the 41 foreigners, some of world renown. For an artist, the familiar can become strange, the strange familiar. A local photographer may have known a certain place all his life. Yet he looks at it with fresh eyes each time he photographs it. There is always a new angle and each picture can say something never said before. When the artist behind the camera is from another land, the object he is seeing for the first time does not remain strange for long — he sees the possibilities and senses its essence. A basic strength of this project is that each photographer is given the field he is best at — aerial, underwater, landscape, wildlife, city streets, rural scenes, tribal life, whatever. They call for some adjusting, of course. Michael Freeman, one of the four foreign writers in this book, ruefully mentions "a novel hazard" for photographers not used to the tropical climate — "a steady stream of perspiration onto and into cameras". The essays — combinations of narration, description, analysis and comment — are illuminating. Though pictures have an instant impact, the essays offer not only useful background information but also some vital insights into this complex country and her multi-ethnic people. It is important that Michael Freeman pays a handsome tribute to the "unsung heroes" of this project — the local people, "the small army of guides, trackers, pilots, boatmen and other helpers" who, for the photographers, were "the ground crew, with years of practical experience". The old photographs of Malaya, Sabah and Sarawak contributed by John Falconer contrast intriguingly with those of contemporary Malaysia, taken nearly a century later. He makes the point that "while superficially we are struck most forcibly by the changes..., at a deeper level what is most moving and inspiring...is the degree of cultural cohesion amid diversity..." We could take this a step further by saying that through significant similarities between the old and the new photographs, we can perhaps find the intangible factor called the Malaysian identity, or Malaysia's 'heart'. Paul Wachtel has written a thoughtful essay highlighting the complex relationship and the intricate network between Nature and Man while providing riveting information about some of the "bewildering variety of life" to which Malaysia is host. Gavin Young's essay, written in his distinctive style, stimulates consciousness of contrasting lifestyles in a changing society. Gone, he notes, are the Malaya and Borneo of Joseph Conrad, Somerset Maugham, Hugh Clifford, Frank Swettenham and the White Rajahs. Malay, Chinese and Indian ways of life are depicted side by side, the contrasts sharpened by brilliant use of detail and the telling phrase. The essays and the captions together provide a frame of reference for the wealth of sensory stimuli supplied by the pictures. The total impact on the senses, the mind and the feelings is quite extraordinary. The wondrous variety that is Malaysia has been captured in a rare combination of truth and beauty. The range is tremendous, covering the sublime and the mundane, the vast wilds and the crowded city, the past and the present with a bold augury of the future. Different cultures co-exist, overlap, enrich one another. Societies in transition combine symbols of various ages. These are portrayed in harsh contrasts or delicate nuances, in a coverage that embraces not only the thriving but also the swiftly vanishing and the gently emerging. To know Malaysia through this book will indeed be to love Malaysia. As in the ancient tale of the spirit-princess of the mountains, here are woven together the most truthful and beautiful elements that make up the heart of Malaysia.

ADIBAH AMIN

1

150 YEARS OF PHOTOGRAPHY IN MALAYSIA

The convergence of nearly 50 photographers, armed with all the paraphernalia of modern technology, with little more than a week in which to encapsulate the whole diversity of the Malaysian scene is a unique event. But unique as it is, it falls into a tradition of documentation within the history of photography in Southeast Asia that stretches back nearly a century and a half.

The sophistication of their equipment – with cameras for specialised applications – might seem at first sight to emphasize the gulf between the photographer of today and his 19th century forebears. But a glance at surviving pictures shows this gulf to be illusory: the photographer's challenge has remained constant despite the advances in chemicals used and optical perfection achieved – it is to capture on film the essence of the visual world.

From the earliest contacts between cultures, photography has sought to illustrate and explain both the differences and points of common contact between peoples with an immediacy denied to the written word. What *is* perhaps unique in this venture is the degree of organisation and co-operation at all levels, from the governmental to the personal which, aided by the infrastructure of modern communications, has enabled such a project to be undertaken. But for the individual photographer on the ground the task remains unchanged: the camera's accuracy and the photographer's vision and sensitivity are united in pursuit of those evanescent images which embody the soul of a country. Whether in a landscape or a portrait, the panoramic view or the minute detail, the art of photography at its finest presents the

most compelling and immediate approximation of reality that we know.

When European navigators in the closing years of the 15th century rounded the Cape of Good Hope, they found a complex and developed network of trade and culture stretching from China in the East to Hormuz at the mouth of the Persian Gulf. Central to this great web of trade was Malacca, strategically placed along the straits controlling the seaways to the east. In the 15th century, Malacca was the centre of a cosmopolitan trading empire, a seat of political and cultural power from which Islam spread outwards to the islands of the archipelago. As a centre of the spice trade, the peninsula fascinated travellers and explorers. The resulting visual documentation of the Southeast Asian states, which can be traced as far back as the 16th century, was to be continued in succeeding decades and centuries.

We do not know the name of the first photographer to visit the Malayan mainland. But it is unlikely that more than a few years elapsed after the public announcement of the invention of photography in 1839 before some traveller utilised the new art in the peninsula. The suitability of photography as a medium of record was quickly appreciated, and travellers immediately set out with cameras to bring back images of distant and exotic lands for European consumption. By the end of 1839 news of photography had reached India and by the early 1840s had spread to the Far East. The *Hikayat Abdullah* describes a daguerreotype being taken in Singapore in around 1841, and

These images of Dayak women were taken at the turn of the century, but the Iban weaver continues her tradition – see *page 165* – and the Kenyah is still husking rice with wooden pestles today.

by 1843 Gaston Dutronquoy was advertising his studio on the island. And it seems likely that from this time on more intrepid photographers would have ventured further afield. By the 1850s Singapore could boast at least one or two professional photographers in residence at any one time, and no doubt many of them followed the example of J Newman, who announced a photographic excursion to Malacca in 1857. For all these early workers, Singapore formed a convenient base from which to mount photographic forays to outlying locations. Thus when the distinguished firm of Sachtler & Co (who had maintained a Penang branch in the mid-1860s) closed down in 1874, among the 1500 glass negatives that were offered for sale at auction were views from Penang, Malacca, Siam, Borneo, Burma and Indo-China. Indeed the firm had sent a lavish album of photographs of the Straits Settlements to the Paris Exhibition of 1867.

In 1867 a German arrived to establish what was to become the most celebrated photographic business in Southeast Asia. Although the firm of GR Lambert and Co's main branch was to remain in Singapore for the half century of its life up to its demise in about 1918, its importance to the documentation of Peninsular Malaya cannot be underestimated. In common with earlier operators based on the island, the firm made trips both to the mainland and throughout the islands of the archipelago. Following the opening up of the Deli region of Sumatra to tobacco cultivation, and a consequent influx of Europeans, a branch studio was set up in Medan in the mid-1880s. Similarly in the peninsula. In 1880 the centre of British administration was transferred from Klang to the rapidly expanding town of Kuala Lumpur. A few years later, in around 1884, photographers from the firm were brought up to make a record of the town at this turning point in its development. The series of views, showing the buildings and streets of early Kuala Lumpur, offers a fascinating point of comparison with photographs of the bustling city of today.

In addition to the sizeable portfolio of commercial views produced to show visitors the landscape and peoples of Malaya, its beauties and economic potential, they also provided a valuable visual reference to events in the political development of the country. This strand of documentary record can be followed through the years, in the work of photographic firms since the mid-19th century who have recorded the growth of a nation from the Independence celebrations of 1957 to the annual festivities which every year mark *Merdeka*.

In 1990 the photographers of *Malaysia, Heart of South-East Asia* have continued that tradition in their own contribution to this documentation.

Inevitably, a medium of of technology brought to Southeast Asia from Europe remained largely under western control in the early days. But this situation changed after a few years, since most European photographers required assistants and these were usually recruited from the local population. From the late 1850s onwards the few records of photographic firms that list all the staff show a fair proportion of Malay, Chinese and Indian assistants working in every capacity from clerks and book-keepers to camera operators. In fact, the attribution of particular photographs to the European who managed the firm is in many cases misleading. We will never know conclusively who actually took the photographs but it is more than likely that many were shot by an unnamed and uncredited local assistant.

Once these assistants had absorbed the technicalities of the photographic craft, it was only a matter of time before they branched out and established businesses of their own, generally at the start catering largely for their own racial groups. From the evidence of surviving but unsigned prints, it seems that a number of Chinese photographers were operating independently within their own community by the 1880s. By the 1890s many of these firms had moved into the mainstream of economic life, and plied their trade successfully in the face of European competition, producing work of comparable standard and apparently patronised as much by the European as by the indigenous population. In this period and from the turn of the century onwards, Chinese firms were on an equal footing with European businesses and were in all the major towns.

In Kuala Lumpur, the business of Kung U was active from at least the early 1900s, as was Bee Wah at 12 Yap Ah Loy Street. Both these photographers issued their portrait and group studies on elaborate coloured and signed mounts, and the volume of their surviving work indicates thriving practices. In Penang the Keechun Studio at 22 Leith Street produced competent work, while in a Kelantan a little later in the century the Kwan Wing Studio made a number of formal portrait studies of the Sultan.

A Japanese presence can be seen in the studios set up in Kuala Kangsar by the Nature Art Studio, and at Muar in the 1920s by P Arita. The most successful of the Japanese photographers was MS Nakajima, who advertised his business as "a photographer and artist, photographic dealers, Japanese curios" based in High Street, Kuala Lumpur from around 1910. The firm also operated a branch at Klang, and survived for several decades, maintaining a staff of fifteen.

Also in Kuala Lumpur two Chinese firms successfully challenged European dominance in the photographic market. The first of these, the Federal Photographic Studio, was at 39 Sultan Street from about 1900 and was managed by Yip Kun and later Ng Kwan Guan. This firm does not appear to have survived much beyond 1906 and its work was absorbed by the Commercial Press and Federal Photographic Studio at 2 Sultan Street in 1908. Under the joint proprietorship of Yuen Ka Tsueng and Yuen Tak Sam, the firm expanded over the years, taking over Number 3 Sultan Street in about 1911. But the flourishing economy that had existed for professional photographers in the early years of the 20th century inevitably declined as improved technology made the medium easy for amateurs to master. By 1916 the business was mainly in supplying equipment and facilities for amateurs rather than taking photographs, and by 1921 the whole photographic side of the business was dropped and Commercial Press henceforward concentrated entirely on printing and publishing.

The subjects most attractive to the photographer have not drastically changed over the period of the medium's presence in Southeast Asia, and this perhaps accounts for something of its fascination, as we compare portraits, scenes and views of a century ago with those taken today. Points of contrast emerge, townscapes evolve and develop, the tools of industry become more sophisticated, costume and culture become more cosmopolitan. But beneath the physical change can be discerned that essential strand of continuity which defines a culture and which photography is uniquely qualified to record. While superficially we are struck most forcibly by the changes that become apparent when comparing photographs separated in time by a century or more, at a deeper level what is most moving and inspiring about these juxtapositions is the degree of cultural cohesion amid diversity that they reveal.

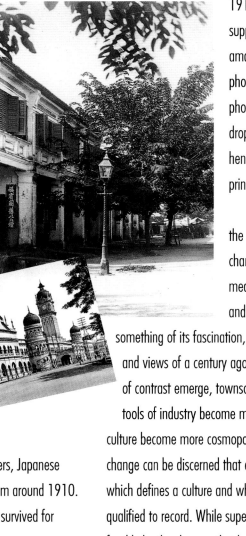

August Kalfuss' view of Third Street in Taiping taken around 1890 and the Sultan Ahmad Samad building in Kuala Lumpur are architectural examples of the cultural diversity of the country.

The work of Charles Kleingrothe supplies the most vivid testimony to the continuity of the photographic challenge over the past century. Moving from Sumatra where he was originally working as a photographic assistant, Kleingrothe travelled the length and breadth of the peninsula in the early years of this century, the results of which are contained in a large portfolio entitled *Malay Peninsula*, published in 1907. Separated in time by over 80 years from this book, it attempted a similar evocation of the spirit of a country as that captured in *Malaysia: Heart of Southeast Asia*, presenting views of major towns and cities, landscape and jungle scenes and the many forms of economic development as well as portraits of the various races and cultures. *Top:* Station Road, Ipoh, in the early 1900s; *bottom:* a Chinese coastal junk moored at Nibong Tebal in Penang. *Preceding:* The Pahang River at Kuala Lipis and the shallow draught boats which navigated it, photographed by Charles Kleingrothe.

any of Charles Kleingrothe's photographs were used in publications of the Malay States Development Agency aimed at publicising the land, people and potential of the country to the outside world, including the picture of Penang's Weld Quay, *top*, which reflected the trade serviced by the busy port and its *tongkangs* or lighters. *Bottom:* The junction of Carpenter Street and Rock Road in Kuching, Sarawak, taken by GR Lambert & Co — the firm which hired Kleingrothe. Much of old Kuching remains unchanged, making it one of the most romantic towns in Southeast Asia.

The man who took these pictures — Charles Hose (1863-1929) — worked for 23 years in the Sarawak Civil Service of Rajah Brooke. During this time he became the undisputed authority on the geography, anthropology and natural history of the state. His books on Sarawak remain standard works to this day. He was perhaps the first photographer who approached the Dayak culture sympathetically and without condescension. *Right:* A Kayan chief and his companion. *Left, clockwise from top:* An Iban woman in traditional finery, with headdress and corset of rattan rings; Lujai, an Ukit man of the Upper Rajang; Kalimantan girl of the Tinjar River wearing heavy copper earrings and decorated cap, and Tama Kulieng or Boi Jolong, a chief of the Batang Kayan River.

Sultan Ahmad Muazzam Shah of Pahang, *left*, photographed in traditional costume with his retinue outside the istana in Pekan in 1885, was founder of the sultanate. Ruling from 1863 to 1914, he proved himself to be one of the most energetic and autocratic of Malay rulers and displayed his military skills most impressively during the uprising of the early 1890s. The Pahang Malay, according to Hugh Clifford, the British Resident, "thinks chiefly of deeds of arms...and is, above all things, manly and reckless...The Pahang boy grows up amid talk of war and rumours of war, which makes him long to be a man that he may use his weapons."

The jewellery and dresses of these Perak women, *left*, photographed in 1903 by GR Lambert & Co — the most famous photographic firm in Southeast Asia at the time — proclaim them to be from the upper class. The woman who is seated was the daughter-in-law of the ruler, Sultan Idris. Her husband, Abdul Jalil, was himself ruler of the state in 1916-18. Her two attendants would also have been drawn from the upper echelon of Malay society.

The Yang di-Pertuan Muda of Trengganu, *far left top*, photographed in front of the istana at Kuala Trengganu in 1909. He ruled briefly as Sultan Muhammad II in 1918-20 before abdicating and moving to Singapore. *Clockwise from left:* Sultan Ismail of Kelantan ruled from 1920 to 1944. This picture was taken in 1931 by Kwan Wing Studio, a Chinese-run business in the state that had royalty among its clientele; Tuanku Abdul Rahman of Negri Sembilan (1895-1960) with his consort Tuanku Ampuan Khursiah, photographed in 1934, shortly after he became Yang di-Pertuan Besar of the state — a position he held until he was elected Yang di-Pertuan Agong of the Federation of Malaya in 1957; Sultan Zainal Abidin III (1864-1918) ruled Kelantan from 1881 and was photographed in 1909 in his palace grounds by GR Lambert & Co when he hosted a visit by the British High Commissioner which resulted in the installation of a British agent. Sir Frank Swettenham called him "a devout" Muslim.

Hee Ngho Chow of Malacca, *right*, photographed in 1904 in his 88th year. Traditional Chinese families often had such photographs taken in the later years of life, showing the subject dressed in Chinese imperial costume. This picture is in the ancestral shrine of a family house in Jonkers Street, Malacca. *Top left:* The mixed attire of this family of the 1930s clearly identifies them as members of the *baba-nonya* or Straits Chinese community. Over a period, this community has absorbed aspects of Malayan and European language, costume, food and architecture, forging a unique cultural identity in Southeast Asia in the process. *Bottom left:* A *baba-nonya* couple in traditional wedding dress, 1950. Although the Straits Chinese had largely stopped wearing their distinctive attire by the end of World War II, the wearing of splendid traditional clothes for special occasions persists to this day.

M a Boey Hon, *right*, a prominent Kuching businessman and friend of the second and third rajahs of Sarawak, had this picture taken at the top of Santubong in 1907. A keen photographer himself, several of his pictures were used in C Baring Gold and CA Bampfylde's *A History of Sarawak Under its Two White Rajahs 1839-1908*. *Top left:* Much of the labour employed in the plantation economy of Malaya in the late 19th century was recruited from southern India. This elegantly posed group of Indian women shows part of the labour force of a plantation in Province Wellesley in the 1880s. *Bottom left:* A Malay group in Sarawak in the early 1890s.

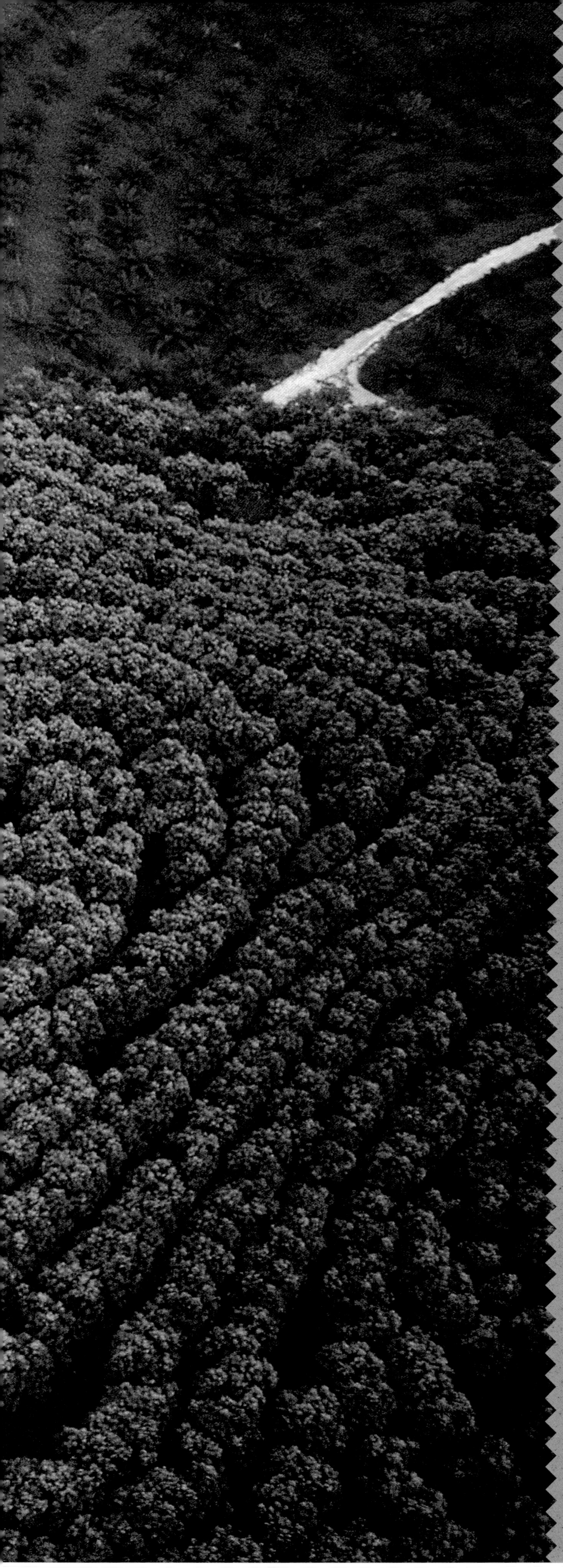

2

NATURE
THE GODDESS WITH A
THOUSAND FACES

Mt Kinabalu is Southeast Asia's tallest mountain at 4,101m, *preceding* and *these pages,* and dominates the landscape of the state of Sabah. It derives its name from the Kadazan *Aki Nabalu* meaning "revered place of the dead" because it is where Kinoingan the Creator lives. The mountain has large enough areas of forest girdling its base to generate its own climate: clouds wrap it in mist but when they are ripped apart momentarily, its peaks — nicknamed Donkey's Ears and Ugly Sister — are revealed, looking like a mangled Swiss army knife.

Mt Kinabalu's highest peak is named after Hugh Low, who reached it in 1851. Falling sheer for 1,500m below the peak is the dramatic Low's Gully, *left*, the greatest drop in Southeast Asia. Several thousand people are drawn to scale Mt Kinabalu each year. Most people take two days to make the climb. The record holder is a Gurkha soldier named Sundar L Kumar who ran up and down in two hours, 29 minutes and 38 seconds.

2

NATURE
THE GODDESS WITH A
THOUSAND FACES

A weak burst of heat lightning illuminates a two-metre leatherback turtle that has plodded ashore to lay her eggs, as her kind have done for millions of years. Where a river meets the sea, a "Dutch monkey" watches a man throws his fishing net. A Penan in the Borneo forest silently lifts his blowpipe to kill a gibbon. A fisherman paints a bird's eye on the prow of his fishing boat to bring good fortune. A visitor, stopping for a rest while climbing Southeast Asia's highest mountain, marvels at a pitcher plant murdering its dinner. An Iban watches the flight of birds along an inland river, and decides not to go to his farm that day. A labourer with a chainsaw sends a towering dipterocarp crashing to earth. A physician prescribes edible birds' nest to treat a persistent cough.

In the city, a businessman pays absolutely no attention to nature at all. It always has been there, always will be. Across town, a state planning official tries to balance the long-term need to keep water flowing in the taps against the state's immediate need for quick cash.

Nature in Malaysia is a Goddess of a thousand faces. People see in her what they wish — vulnerability, majesty, food, a cosmic balance, spirits... People look at Nature and see themselves — warrior, hunter, hustler, voyager, parent, student, poet.

Nature has blessed Malaysia. The country's geography, climate and varying topography have created a natural feast. Because Malaysia has such a wide variety of environments — forests, wetlands, mountains and seas, it hosts a bewildering variety of life.

Malaysia has the big animals — tiger, sun bears, tapirs, Sumatran rhinos, wild cattle. And it has the enigmatic — ancient

Dennis Lau

Jean-Paul Ferrero

sea turtles and giant smelly flowers. Ungainly hornbills and delicate sunbirds. And then there is the bright blue-metallic coloured beetle with a cherry-red racing stripe down its back. It lives in the rainforest of Taman Negara. Alfred Russel Wallace, the famous Victorian naturalist, found 2,000 different kinds of beetles in a single square mile of forest in what is now Peninsular Malaysia.

Malaysia's rainforests are among the oldest on earth, and have evolved a variety of life that befuddle scientists. Scientists can safely guess that perhaps 60 percent of all the earth's species live in the rainforests. But how many is that? Scientists simply do not know. At a minimum, five million. Maximum? Ten? Thirty? Fifty? Perhaps one hundred million species of things? This is astounding enough — that there are so many different creatures. What makes it even more bewildering is the likelihood that most of these yet-to-be-discovered things are beetles. "God has an inordinate fondness for beetles," said a biologist once.

Why does the earth need so many different things? Why are there 100 species of frogs in Malaysia, and not 10? Why are there so many types of monkeys? By what master plan does Borneo contain 11,000 plant species, about one in every 20 in the world? Why does a Malaysian rainforest have up to 180 different species of trees in one hectare while a temperate forest of similar size would probably have less than 10? It has something to do with changing sea levels. But it is also pleasing to have variety. It fulfills a basic need for difference. It maintains mystery, it generates curiosity, it inspires.

For this young Penan girl living in the forests of Sarawak, nature's bounty and man's livelihood — which involves cutting down the trees — is a crucial and often complex relationship. *Preceding:* Rubber is not native to Malaysia, but in the West Coast, it dominates the landscape and remains a major commodity in Malaysia's lists of exports.

Mt Kinabalu is known, to most visitors, as a rock. A big rock. The highest rock between the Himalayas and the island of New Guinea. As rocks go, Mt Kinabalu at 4,101m, or 13,455 ft, is honest in appearance, although hardly pretty. Its top ridges jag and point into the sky; peaks with names like Donkey's Ears and Ugly Sister form the outline of a mangled Swiss army knife, all broken blades and twisted can openers.

Tom Harrisson, former curator of the Sarawak Museum and never one to flee from hyperbole, stood in awe of Mt Kinabalu, deciding that "surely this is the most complete statement of 'I am a mountain' made anywhere on this earth." To support that view, Harrisson noted that during World War II, American pilots flying over Sabah said, "that Goddamned thing cannot be 13,000 ft. Why, that's nothing. It must be near as high as Mt Everest. These Borneo maps are to hell anyway." And so the airmen elevated Borneo's highest mountain to a more respectable 19,000 ft.

As rocks go, Mt Kinabalu is big enough, and has sufficiently vast areas of forest girdling its base to generate its own climate. Clouds wrap the mountain in mist, then disappear to reveal gnarled dwarf forests with molten-green moss dripping from withered branches. Within minutes the clouds encircle the massif again. Then the curtain of clouds is ripped apart, giving tantalising glimpses of teeth and fangs. Finally the clouds shudder. Enough revelation for this afternoon. They smother the black mountain, at this moment, at least, in a shroud of white.

This is a rock of life, and of death. It is a rock, a granite pluton to be precise, where the spirits of ancestors live and the lives of mere mortals are determined. It dominates the landscape and psyche of the state of Sabah, and challenges the stamina of about one-sixth of the 200,000 annual visitors to Kinabalu National Park. To most climbers, Mt Kinabalu is a challenge, something to "conquer". This is a good thing. People need physical challenges to discover their own limits. (Most people take two days. The record holder is a Gurkha named Sundar L Kumar who ran up and down in 2 hours, 29 minutes and 38 seconds during the 1989 Kinabalu Climbathon.) And, having woken before dawn on the second day in order to reach the summit by sunrise, the pilgrims of the physical are treated to a magical view of the sun as it eases its way over the Philippines, slides around an outcrop and over a ravine one and a half kilometres deep. Finally one begins to see distinctive shapes, a garden of rock, gulleys and caverns, outcrops and vast open fields of grey that are lit pink by the dawn. This, to most people, is sufficient compensation for the pain.

But to those people who stop panting long enough to look around, it is one of the world's most important botanical gardens, where life and death occur in dramatic fashion. A pitcher plant kills for its dinner, first by seduction, then by drowning.

Danson Kandaung, a guide at Kinabalu National Park, encourages a visitor to look more closely at the floristic carnivore. "This is *Nepenthes kinabaluensis*," he says, taking hikers five metres off the well-worn trial in order to point out a reddish pitcher plant. "It's a natural hybrid between *Nepenthes rajah* and *Nepenthes villosa*." The pitcher and its "hat" are formed by a leaf gone wild, the young guide explains. The

The forms of Malaysia's natural beauty: ferns and touch-me-not mimosas convey a feeling of lushness. The lotus, rising from the mud, is a symbol of beauty in the midst of impurity.

inside of the pitcher is filled with a deadly potion of water and digestive juices which attract thirsty and curious insects. Once inside, the ill-fated invertebrate finds that the walls are slippery and, even if it makes it to the top of the pitcher, its path is blocked by inward-pointing spikes. The insect drowns and is digested, giving off a powerful smell of decay.

Why can't pitcher plants live normal photosynthetic lives like other plants? The main reason is they live on very poor soil. They need to get their nutrition from external sources. And because plants are stationary, they have to be clever enough to entice the dinner to come to them. The scientific name *Nepenthes* comes from a Greek word meaning "removing sorrow"; Homer, in his *Odyssey* refers to Helen adding drugs to wine in order to relieve the grief of men.

Kinabalu National Park is home to nine species of pitcher plants, ranging from the hourglass-shaped *Nepenthes lowii* to the giant *Nepenthese rajah*. One *N. rajah* was found to contain four litres of liquid while a second was digesting a drowned rat. The local name for pitcher plants, perhaps acknowledging their often formidable size, is *periok kera* or "monkeys' cooking pots." This is impressive biological diversity, but it represents just a fraction of Kinabalu's vegetation.

On Mt Kinabalu can also be found the sunshine yellow flowers of *Rhododendron lowii*, one of 26 rhododendron species found in the national park, which is Malaysia's most visited. Largely due to the park's altitude variations, ranging from lowland rainforest at 152 metres to more than 4,000 metres, Mt Kinabalu boasts varieties of virtually all plant families. There are some 450 species of ferns. And there is *Rafflesia arnoldii*.

Sir Stamford Raffles and Dr Joseph Arnold are credited with discovering this plant in Sumatra in 1818, hence the name. (Scientists have subsequently discovered 13 other species of *Rafflesia*, all in Southeast Asia.) The *Rafflesia* is the world's biggest flower, sometimes reaching a metre in width. It may bud for anywhere from nine months to a year and a half before bursting into bloom, its flower may then last just a few days. It is parasitic, and, in spite of its size, its pre- and post-flower forms are modest. Junaidi Payne, of the World Wide Fund for Nature, noted in his book *Wild Malaysia* that "from a distance the buds resemble pale orange cabbages wrapped in a charred newspaper, while dead flowers look like pieces of a tyre inner tube." Of more interest, perhaps, to those interested in preserving the good name of Mr Raffles is the fact that local people call *Rafflesia* the "stinking corpse lily", because of its distinctive odour. Perhaps Raffles, himself an exceptional naturalist, might have preferred being the namesake for *Amorphophallus titanum*, so named because it boasts the world's tallest flower.

But, just as yin opposes yang, there would have been a flip side to that honour as well. Like *Rafflesia*, *Amorphophallus* too smells of carrion, a useful way for the stationary plant to attract flies which act as pollinators. The casual visitor has to work hard to see these dramatic plants. Jamili Nais, Sabah Parks botanist, notes that in all of Sabah there are only 25 *Rafflesia* sites left and that most of the host plants are found in prime timber areas.

Where some people see beauty, others see cash. Borneo accounts for 10 percent of the world's orchids, about 3,000 species, with at least 1,500 to 2,000 growing in Sabah. Many of these are rare and sought after by collectors worldwide. Headlined the Kota Kinabalu *Daily Express* of 26 June 1989: "Kinabalu Park among places believed 'raped' by botanist" — a "rare orchid" smuggler, Armenian-born Briton Henry Azadehel, had been sentenced to a year's jail in Britain and fined £20,000 for smuggling the rare, and protected, *Paphiopedilum rothschildianum* into the country.

Mt Kinabalu's vegetation, its mist, its altitude, its beauty has another benefit for mankind — water. Mt Kinabalu receives some five metres of rain a year; from the hills of this wet rock flow eight rivers. These provide water for farming for many of

Sabah's people. Which leads us, indirectly, to the question of ancestors. First of all, one has to be willing to consider the existence of spirits. If one believes that every person has a spirit, then the spirit must go somewhere when the body dies. What more fitting transit lounge then this giant living rock, swirled in cloud, inaccessible, towering above the plains?

Up to a generation ago local Kadazans were buried facing Mt Kinabalu. To make it easier for their souls to have a non-stop flight to the rock, conscientious mourners buried a bamboo pole next to the deceased's head, with the exposed portion of the bamboo pointing in the direction of the mountain's summit. Many anthropologists believe that the name "Kinabalu" is a variation on the Kadazan words "Aki Nabalu", which mean "revered place of the dead". When early explorers tackled the mountain the native guides insisted that white hens be first sacrificed to propitiate the ancestors and gods who lived on the misty rock. Today, some of the older guides in Kinabalu National Park make an annual sacrifice, although young Christians such as Danson rarely take part.

Nik Wheeler

William Waterfall

According to Kadazan tradition, Kinoingan, the Creator and Almighty God lives on Mt Kinabalu, with the ancestral spirits. In this way traditional religion, ancestor worship, mythology and pragmatism merge. Nature, in the form of Mt Kinabalu and the forests surrounding it, equals water. Water, in the form of rain and rivers, equals food. Food equals life. So Nature equals life. A reasonable concept to ponder while saying a brief prayer to one's own ancestors during a walk on the rock.

Bats need a better press agent. To most people these flying creatures, by far the most populous group of mammals in Malaysia, are symbols of evil and destruction, dark and mysterious. In fact, the 10 million bats found in the Deer Cave in Sarawak's Gunung Mulu National Park form one of nature's most efficient clean-up squads, eating an estimated three tons of insects each day.

Ecologists call the insect-eating done by bats "an environmental service", and encourage government planners to take difficult-to-evaluate benefits of nature like these into account when calculating the value of a natural area. At sunset each day, a visitor sitting in the comfortable Bat Observatory opposite the (small) apartment building-sized entrance to Deer Cave notices a ribbon-like stream of black creatures, a wavering, pulsating tornado of bats that quits the cave and twists through the air in search of dinner. Their flight sounds like the wind, a precursor to a storm. Where the bats fly in front of foliage the trees shimmer with life, like a heat reflection. The first stream of bats lasts five minutes, followed by a second, a fifth, a tenth, until finally the bats fly out continuously for an hour and a half, commuting just as resolutely as the urban businessmen who clog the world's highways each morning and evening.

A walk into the bats' dark home, along the well-developed walkway inside the Deer Cave, leads to a subterranean river that flows into a fairly inaccessible verdant valley. Dubbed the Garden of Eden by Mulu explorers, this glen, surrounded on all sides by sheer limestone cliffs, is bright and lush, a welcome relief from the dark and dank of the cave. The garden is fresh and smells of life, in contrast to the bat and swiftlet guano of the cave that

Mt Kinabalu looms over the city that bears its name: Kota Kinabalu, which means "the City of Kinabalu". Malaysia's beauty, and the Western dream of palm-fringed tropical beaches are what draw tourists to the country.

Just a few dozen kilometres away, in the Sepilok Nature Reserve, a seven-year-old orangutan named BJ approaches a visitor sitting under a tree. BJ is a "rehabilitant", an unfortunate word that describes the dozens of apes at Sepilok who were captured for the pet trade and then confiscated by Malaysian officials, or who were orphaned when their forest home was cleared for oil palm plantations or timber. BJ shuffles on the ground, walking upright with his red arms hanging almost to his ankles. He sits down and leans over the man's shoulder, watching him scribble notes. "I can teach you to write, BJ," the man optimistically says, half expecting the ape to respond. He and BJ engage in a deep, meaningful stare. "This is how you write your name." The man writes the initials. BJ's chin is on the man's shoulder. Before the man can finish another letter, BJ rips the notebook out of his hands, sticks it in his mouth and scampers up a tree.

BJ reminds one of the comments of Malcolm MacDonald, former governor-general of colonial Malaya and Borneo, who thought that "these members of the order Primates contemplate you, when you meet them, with melancholy eyes, as if they had just read Darwin's *Origin of Species* and were painfully aware of being your poor relations who have not done so well in life."

BJ and his orangutan buddies are clearly intelligent, even human-like. But are there even more human-like creatures in the Sabah forest? A new species of bat was discovered recently in Sepilok. A small step for science, perhaps, but it indicates that in Sabah's rainforests scientists still have many frontiers to explore. For one thing, the experts have yet to produce a *batutut*.

"My father ran a plantation in Tuaran, near Kota Kinabalu," a Sandakan-based travel agent named Patricia explained. "People cut a road in the hill where the little people live. They were furious, and caused all sorts of trouble." Patricia is describing a *batutut*, also called *orang pendek* or short person. Most reports of these creatures border on the incredulous, but there are enough reports of this tropical *yeti* to give one pause.

Although the scientific community scoffs at sightings of *untrahoms* (unidentified tropical Asian hominoids), the local people are well acquainted with them, which is why they give them names. And enough respected authorities have collected evidence throughout Southeast Asia of these strange creatures to at least give pause to the skeptics.

Untrahoms clearly evoke visceral reactions in many people. For rural villagers, they may symbolise man's rejection of his animal nature, an age-old conflict of a species whose culture sets it apart from its closest relatives. Yet this separation is always somewhat ambivalent, as people both deny their jungle essence and secretly savour it. People are fascinated by discoveries of fossil hominids and avidly devour reports of the field studies of gorillas, chimpanzees, and orangutans. The great apes are among the most popular zoo exhibits. But most people are uncomfortable when they get too close to their animal selves. Animal-like behaviour is frowned upon. Throughout Malaysia, as in other parts of Asia, special emphasis is placed on making sure that people act like humans, not like wild beasts.

Michelangelo Durazzo

William Waterfall

Giant tree ferns, buttress roots, and a thousand subtle hues and textures make the Malaysian forest a place of great beauty for those who take the trouble to explore it on its own terms.

Among Asia's forest people who are in daily contact with 'wild nature', the various forms of untrahoms are an ever-present reminder of what it means to be man-like, yet not human. Untrahoms live in the forest, away from people who fear and respect both them and their forest home. The *batutut* is said to kill people before ripping out their livers.

Myths and legends of giants and ape-men have survival value for mankind. As the British philosopher Angus Hall suggests: "We need creatures like these to inhabit that strange borderland between fact and fantasy, and our interest lies not so much in whether they really exist but in the possibility that they may exist." Yet, the great forest areas which shelter untrahoms — be they the *batutut* of Sabah, the *beruang rambai* of Sarawak, the *Uyan* of Pahang, the *sedapa* of Sumatra, the *ye rin* of China or the *tua yeua* of Thailand — are fast being sold to timber concessionaires, chopped into smaller fragments, or cleared by shifting cultivators. Rural people, who define their humanity both by

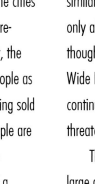

Jean-Paul Ferrero

what they are and what they are not, are moving to the cities or large villages and the concept of humanity is being re-defined. Instead of being the home of the human spirit, the rainforest is often considered by the educated urban people as unproductive wilderness that can best serve man by being sold for timber and the land used to grow oil palm. City people are too sophisticated to consider that the destruction of the untrahom's rainforest habitat takes away the home of a relative we will probably never meet in person.

But Sepilok has other mysteries, more fathomable, and perhaps more directly relevant to human survival. The forest rewards those who venture into it. Sepilok has one of the most attractive forests in Malaysia, and one of the richest. Park Ranger Joseph Radin stopped by the Sepilok forest path and walked into the underbush. "This giant fern is *Faspalum nidus*. Local people make a medicine from it that helps people with trouble breathing…The Japanese asked us to send five kilograms to a lab in Japan."

Around the world more than 6,000 plants are regularly used in traditional, folk and herbal medicine. The Geneva-based World Health Organisation sees traditional medicine as providing the primary health care of 80 percent of the people in the developing world. As Harvard professor Richard Evans Schultes (the "father of ethnobotany") puts it: "Through most of man's history, botany and medicine were, for all practical purposes, synonomous fields of knowledge." Skeptics may scoff that many traditional medicines are worthless but 74 percent of the plant-derived chemicals currently prescribed in the west were used by other societies for similar purposes long before their discovery by science. So far, only about 10,000 of the 250,000 species of flowering plants thought to exist have been thoroughly screened. Yet the World Wide Fund for Nature estimates that, if current destruction rates continue, some 60,000 plants, one in four, will be extinct or threatened by the year 2050.

The mysteries in this forest are the mysteries of life. Animals, large and small, play out their stories, unaware of man but influenced by him. The Goddess perhaps looks on. Is she smiling?

Jean-Paul Ferrero

The hornbill is a bird bound in Iban legend and is easier to locate — by virtue of the noise it makes — in the Sarawak jungle than the elusive frogs or toads of which there are some 100 species.

Jean-Paul Ferrero

Perched like circus tight-rope performers, collectors of edible birds' nests scrape the ceilings of the Gomantong Caves in Sabah, *opposite*. Made out of the saliva of swiftlets, the virtually tasteless nests can command up to US$3,500 a kilo when exported to Hong Kong and Singapore. The Chinese use them in soups for therapeutic purposes — a traditional belief partly borne out by research revealing they contain enzymes which can regenerate blood and other cells.

Jean-Paul Ferrero

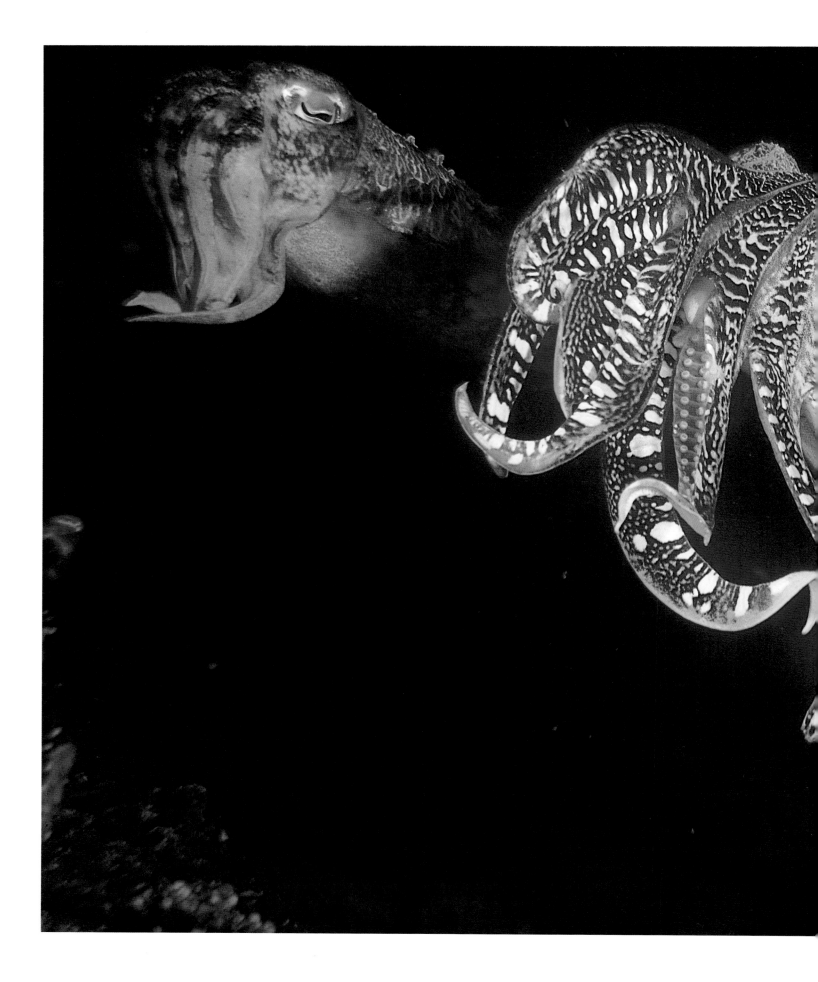

Herwarth Voigtmann

Squid and cuttlefish are common in Southeast Asian waters, and are caught for food and to serve as fish bait. Collectively known as *sotong*, they are an important part of the diet of many Malaysians. The deeper waters of the region are home to larger squids, including some recorded to be 14 metres long, making them by far the largest of the invertebrate animals.

Tommy Chang

Herwarth Voigtmann

The Sabah coast is a paradise for sport divers and marine biologists. After rainforests, coral reefs are the second most diverse ecosystems on earth. Scientists have discovered other riches in the world's coral reefs, particularly medical compounds "so unusual that it would be difficult to dream them up in a lab," according to the *Wall Street Journal*. A drug created from a potent poison that sea sponges use to protect themselves can help arthritis sufferers. A new class of anti-inflammatory drugs are derived from the defensive sting of a fernlike soft coral known as a sea whip. More immediately productive are the oysters, *bottom right*, cultivated in 1,295 hectares of sea water off Pulau Bohey Dulang, the only pearl farm in Malaysia. Between eight and 50kg of cultured pearls are harvested annually and exported to Japan. The Kaya Pearl Co uses X-rays to inspect the pearls being cultivated in the oysters, raising the cages from the sea by means of manually-operated winches.

Tommy Chang

M angroves, *opposite,* are among the earth's most prolific environments, rich in biological diversity and home to silver-leaf monkeys, *top left,* and a number of species of crabs, including the *Uca dussumieri,* a bright blue creature, *bottom left.* The crabs feed on organic matter left by the tides on the muddy tidal flats. They hide in burrows when the tide is in. Mangroves are important breeding grounds for fish and prawns and are crucial to high value/high risk aquaculture, which has great potential serving markets in Singapore, Japan, Europe and the United States.

Slim Sreedharan

Slim Sreedharan

Malaysia is an avian paradise. The pied hornbill *above*, and the purple heron, *right*, found in the Sepilok Nature Reserve in Sabah, have diametrically different nesting habits. The female hornbill builds her nest in a hollow tree and then plasters herself inside, using a mud and droppings mixture which hardens into impenetrable clay. The male, her mate for life, serves her fruit through the narrow slit of the nest during her confinement. In contrast, the purple heron avoids the forest, preferring reed-covered swamps. The male collects the dead reeds for the nest which the female constructs on a platform of reed debris.

t's not known where Malaysia's *Orang Asli,* or 'original people' came from. Estimates of the Orang Asli population put their number at only 35,000, although some sources say they are twice that figure. They comprise 18 tribes that fall into three main groups — the *Senoi,* the Proto-Malays and the Negritos (the last being the smallest and oldest Orang Asli). In the Cameron Highlands, many *Senoi* have become wage earners, working on the tea estates. The one pictured *left,* lives in Malaysia's national park, Taman Negara, where he sometimes acts as a tracker for visitors. Here, he fishes in the Tembeling River.

Karl Ammann

The intrepid adventurer Isabella Bird described the Malayan jungle thus: "Oh that you could see it all! Mr Darwin says so truly that a visit to the tropics is like a visit to a new planet...To realise an equatorial jungle one must see it in all its wonderment of activity and stillness..." Malaysia's first, and arguably most important, national park, Taman Negara, which sprawls across Pahang, Trengganu and Kelantan, is exactly what 'Birdie' saw.

Left: Peninsular Malaysia's numerous rivers frequently break into waterfalls which provide a refreshing change from the stifling heat in the rainforest.

Abdullah Hamzah

Malaysia boasts some one hundred species of frogs and toads. Many rarely leave the security of the primary forest branches, like this tree frog which is difficult to find, *opposite*. It spends most of its time in the holes filled with rain water. Of the world's 5,000 snake species (116 of which live in tropical rainforests), less than one percent are dangerous to people. This extremely poisonous but beautiful Wagler's pit viper, *bottom left*, for example, much prefers squirrels, rats and frogs. Another colourful denizen of the forest is the greater green leafbird, *top left*, whose rich and varied song is usually much fuller in volume than the shama or magpie robin. *Overleaf:* In Sarawak's Bako National Park, a green grass whip snake has made a killing. Surprisingly, it let go of its green-crested lizard prey shortly after this photograph was taken. Perhaps it was put off by the attention of the photographer...

Slim Sreedharan

73

Proboscis monkeys in Sabah, *these pages*, are called *Orang belanda* or 'Dutch men' — not simply because these primates have cucumber-like noses or because the males keep harems of up to ten females. The epithet *belanda* is often used to refer to things exotic or strange from the local point of view. Potbellied and white-tailed, proboscis monkeys are leaf-eaters, flourishing along river banks in mangrove forests.

Jean-Paul Ferrero

Slim Sreedharan

At feeding time the orangutans at the Sepilok Nature Reserve, *these pages*, put on a show. The objective of Sepilok and a similar centre — Semongok — in Sarawak is to 'rehabilitate' once-captive or orphaned orangutans, to life in the forest. Many of the more than 200 orangutans who have passed through Sepilok have, in fact, returned to life in the Sabah rainforest. When young, they move spectacularly through the forest, *overleaf*, but as they grow older they can become very heavy, and move more cautiously.

ff the coast of Sandakan
in Semporna Bay, Sabah,
lie hundreds of islands,
their shores littered with
debris from timber
operations inland. These
islands and their waters
offer refuge to holiday-
makers. Sabah fishermen
know that the coral reefs
are fine fishing grounds,
and the sandy beaches
welcome sea turtles which
come ashore to lay their
eggs. Some turtle sites are
protected by their isolation,
others by government
decree.

Alberto Cassio

Bernard Hermann

The highlands of Bareo, Sarawak, only came to the attention of the English during World War II, when they were identified in an aerial survey. Isolated by rough terrain, Bareo is full of irrigated ricefields, *above*, standing out from the monotony of the surrounding forest. Other treasures are hidden in the great forests of Sabah and Sarawak, like this waterfall, *right*, and the steep limestone cliffs and pinnacles of Mulu National Park, *overleaf*.

3

A SEARCH FOR THE
SOUL OF MALAYSIA

The palm forests run off to the horizon in endless vistas and mysterious gloom through which small birds flicker like green or turquoise chips of jade in stray shafts of sunlight. Bananas rustle their big ragged leaves; slender areca palms shoot graceful trunks like rockets towards the sky and silently explode there in a neat burst of green; and the green top-knots of the coconut trees huddle anxiously round the busy houses of the Malay kampongs because, as is well known, coconuts do not grow with any pleasure beyond the sound of human voices.

Malaysia is one of those places on earth which it is hard not to describe as magical. Hugh Clifford, a Malay-speaking 23-year-old, knew this scenery very well. When he was told by his boss, the British Governor of the Straits Settlements in Singapore, that his immediate future career would henceforth lie in the State of Pahang in the Malay Peninsula, he wrote ecstatically in his diary: "The moon has fallen into my lap" — *Bulan sudah jatuh ke riba*, a common Malay saying.

Clifford — later to become the Straits Governor himself and incidentally a close friend of Joseph Conrad — received his good news in 1887. Even then he had begun worrying about the 'weakening' effect of British influence on the Malays in their truculent, 'untamed' state unsullied by European vulgarity. True, so far the relatively few British officials up-country had had limited cultural influence. Usually they had to be shipped back to Singapore fairly soon, shuddering with fever. Malay life had been little ruffled by the fever-heated breath of European progress. Clifford was horribly aware of its inevitable approach.

Jean-Noël Reichel

Did he foretell the British success in making Malays feel truly Malay? Malays took their time in thinking of themselves as simply 'Malays' rather than, say, 'Kedah Malays' or 'Pahang Malays' and so on, according to state. Perhaps only with the formation by the British of the Malay Regiment in 1930 did soldiers, at least, suddenly begin to think of themselves as 'Malays'. The Japanese occupation no doubt helped. And immediately after that, London's insensitive idea of turning Peninsular Malaya into a colony run from Whitehall. Even old colonial hands like Frank Swettenham wrote angry letters to *The Times* about that folly which finally roused Malays to demand an independent Federation free from Whitehall or anywhere else. This came, without bloodshed, in 1957. In 1963, the Federation of Malaya joined with Sabah and Sarawak and, until 1965, Singapore to form Malaysia. *Tria juncta in uno* (three joined in one) could have been, but somehow was not, the new states' motto.

Malayness still survives today at its most potent and prideful where it has survived for centuries: in the kampongs. Thousands of Malays — Bumiputras, Sons of the Soil, they and the indigenous peoples of East Malaysia are called by the government in Kuala Lumpur, earning certain rights thereby — work in the cities alongside other Malaysians, the Chinese and Indians. But in the Muslim holiday of Hari Raya that ends the fasting month of Ramadan, the exodus reverses itself. Happily they stream home, to the kampongs for family feasting and fun.

What exactly is a kampong? Few are the same in every detail, but I suppose one should start with the foliage which hardly

In the tiny fishing village of Beserah, north of Kuantan on the east coast of the Peninsula, Chinese children grow up alongside Malays, an example of the country's multi-racial culture. *Preceding:* In Sarawak's longhouse communities, young girls grow up like their counterparts elsewhere, hankering after pop music and jeans.

changes. In an emerald landscape, heavy palms, slender areca stems, big-leaved breadfruit, floppy, dark green mangoes, shade-bearing tamarinds and half a hundred other flowering or useful trees huddle at the edge of a track or road. Probably a stream runs through the string of half-seen stilted houses whose roofs poke out of the greenness. Washing like banners hang between verandahs. Ducks paddle, women wash their clothes and their bawling children. There is a smell of curry; a nose-crinkling smell of over-ripe durian fruit. Idle mynah birds stalk about like cockney workmen, cheekily whistling; overhead, a hawk is scouting for mice. Babies with few or no clothes on toddle among chickens with too few feathers. Men stroll or loll in sarongs and singlets, smoking. Others sit cross-legged, eating. All around the sun beats down on the countryside, fertile, often flat, against a background of blue mountains half-lost in a grey-blue haze. There will be a cheap market full of everything. No one can starve in a kampong.

Gerald Gay

Gerald Gay

Another Malaysian world enters the picture when we come to the road. These are the kind of signs that will bombard you: Filem Fuji, Kim Yoke Tan Workshop Ltd, Chee Chuan Sawmills, Sharp, Syme Tyres. Probably there'll be a couple of Chinese chophouses, and a Muslim Indian restaurant. This is multiracial Malaysia putting in an appearance.

When I asked in the course of this modest inquiry where above all I should look for what one might call the "Soul of Malay Malaysia", the answer came back without a pause: "The East Coast." Kelantan, that meant, and Trengganu.

Yet, as a matter of fact, the earliest traces of Malay civilisation have been dug up in Kedah, in the northwest of Malaysia. Jars, bowls and cups, stone caskets hidden in the granite bases of truncated temples are there to be seen in a museum. The point is that Kedah (*Katha* in Sanskrit) was a commercial trading point between South China and India and the Red Sea, just as on the East Coast of the Peninsula (Kelantan and Patani, the state that then lay to its north) was on another trade route linking Java and Cambodia. Thus traces of Thai and Cham influences are to be seen in traditional dances of Kelantan to this day.

The thing about the east coast is that it had always been isolated by the seasonal storms of the northeast monsoon and until recently, difficult land communications, except to the north. Thus arts and crafts, music and dance, the making of kites and tops, and beautiful gold-threaded *kain songket* have survived there. The kingdom of Patani above Kelantan remained Thai, but Kelantan, Trengganu, Perlis and Kedah became British protectorates in 1909. Nevertheless Kelantan Malays still speak in a baffling argot which puzzles Malays from Kuala Lumpur no end.

The jungle folk of Malaysia are another matter. They have been here longest of all. In the dense interior of the Peninsula that extends like a slender leaf into the tepid and shallow seas, among the tangle of dividing ridges of mountain and jungle, riven by few tracks but many watercourses, live perhaps 35,000 of the gentle Orang Asli — the original ones — surviving on what the jungles provide, shunning possessions as they have done for more than 6,000 years. Their fate can be regarded as enviable — or tragic. For these humane, shy people were the first possessors of the East with all its possibilities and riches, but by their nature and circumstance could use none of them. They lived on in the deep jungle, fleeing from strangers, a prey sometimes to the tiger, that fearsome creature they knew as "He with the Hairy Face", cherishing immemorial customs and superstitions; fearing to laugh when a butterfly flutters by (a coincidence that brought a family appalling luck), or unable to count up to more than three after which any number became simply 'many'. Now the Orang Asli are offered schools, jobs, and the vote, and some have swapped bark-cloths, loincloths and bamboo blowpipes for the unimaginative uniform of Western and Eastern youth — skirts, T-shirts, blue jeans.

From the Wild West to the Big Time is how one recent travel guide to Malaysia described Kuala Lumpur, Malaysia's capital. Founded by the gods of Tin, it was later handed over when the metal had made the city rich to British and Federal bureaucrats. When I first saw it years ago it didn't strike me as the "Wild West". It was pleasantly "East". You emerged into its rainy warmness through the oddest, neo-Moghul portal, the entrance to the railway station, and were at once surrounded by other offshoots of the Emperor Babur's Agra or Edwin Lutyens' New Delhi: minarets, crenellated parapets, carved doors. Administrative buildings had arched windows and copper domes and the Supreme Court had black ones like the caps judges put on before pronouncing the death sentence. Across a cricket ground vaguely Tudor buildings hid the Long Bar of the Selangor Club. And nearby the busy Chinese barmen at the Coliseum Bar and Grill dispensed countless gin pahits — pink gins, once the drink of all Eastern Hands and Royal Naval officers — as they had

been doing since 1921. Kuala Lumpur retained something of the air of Somerset Maugham's *The Letter.*

To me it still does. Its half-gracious, half-rough-and-tumble Maughamesque heart is to be found behind the glasses of Tiger Beer in the Coliseum (I seemed to be the only one drinking pink gins). The station still pines for Lahore. The Supreme Court still threatens death (for drug-smuggling). There are McDonalds and discos but also a new and noble mosque, and a National Museum that should be visited. And there are of course those inevitable signs of the "Big Time": the skyscrapers — icing sugar towers, and hard-edged and shiny dominoes announcing Money. Many are hotels. One looks like an elegant tube of toothpaste squeezed in the middle. It is a long time ago since the old Merlin and the Federal were the only hotels de luxe. There were no karaoke bars then.

Above all, Kuala Lumpur remains small and friendly. Do not compare it with Singapore, Bangkok or Jakarta. The comparison is, say, with Brisbane or Bristol. It is inextricably multi-racial; it is utterly non-violent; it is tolerant and at street level quite without racial rancour. That it is socially safe as houses implies a very considerable maturity among its mixture of Chinese, Indian and Malay inhabitants that does not always extend to its politicians. It is important these days to state that while Malaysia is officially a Muslim country, Islam here can be called Islam with a Loving Face. Of course without that grown-up tolerance Malaysia, such a land of minorities, could hardly expect to survive very long. Perhaps it helps that Kuala Lumpur, though

Rene Burri

This Indian girl in Johor mixes modern and traditional styles in typical Malaysian fashion. She wears her hair short while sporting a traditional nose ornament and a trendy watch and is just a part of the polyglot society reflected in the colourful annual National Day parade.

the Federal capital, is small enough to be in touch with the countryside of Malaysia. From its streets, lined with snow-white frangipani or scarlet Flame of the Forest trees, you can look up through the high-rise clusters to the even higher fog-lined ridges, jungle trees and the dramatic outcrops of rock where the heart of Malaysia lies.

I took my first steps in search of Kedah's relics of Old Malaysia with Kamaruddin Zakaria, the chirpy curator of the museum at Merbok, a tiny village, south of Alor Star. Kamaruddin is youngish and giggles a lot. There is nothing of the dry and solemn scholar in Kamaruddin. He wore glasses, a red shirt, and smart white slacks and was radiantly in his element after nine years there contemplating the same relatively few relics. The museum is modern and stands in a well-watered garden of thickish grass and well-ordered trees that climb up a steep slope of Mount Kedah.

Hindu and Buddhist traders eons ago had established a post among the indigenous Malays who lived here, and together they built a town of wooden houses of which nothing at all survives. Because the seashore has much receded since that remote time, nothing remains of what must have been a thriving port. We looked down the slope to the sea, now some way away, and Kamaruddin said: "The ships coming from India and Ceylon carried shale as ballast. Unloaded it somewhere here before filling their ships with cargo; timber, rattans, sandalwood, and such. Unfortunately, that hugh pile of shale has vanished." He gave a regretful giggle.

We are talking about the time between the 4th and the 14th century, and in that time the sea had swept everything away. What major relics there are — and there are a lot of these yet to be dug — are temples. Or rather the hollow bases of temples, once perhaps 30 to 40 feet high, made of granite and laterite stones, sometimes bricks but topped with perishable wood. The stones were chiselled out of the mountain: hence its name Bukit Batu Pahat, the Hill of Chiselled Stone.

"No bones," said Kamaruddin with a merry laugh. "No bodies, no skulls either. Perhaps they burned them. Only the relics in stone caskets hidden below the temple bases." They were tiny things, these relics; Kamaruddin had a collection. Bulls and a number of lingams in gold leaf as thin as cigarette paper. Other bigger things were shown in the museum. Granite lions, for instance, and a mysterious Sanskrit inscription saying "I acknowledge the enemies of the contented King Romarrtha and the wicked are ever afflicted".

"Who is King Romarrtha? Who is he?" said Kamaruddin, stepping with a giggle through a clutch of four-foot high stone lingams, "that is the question. No answer, you see."

In the garden we mounted flights of steps to reach one of the temple bases. Its black stones were round and pitted. "Lava?"

"Gran-**ite**!" Kamaruddin corrected me breezily. We stood under the imposing shoulder of Mount Kedah among bamboos, flowering shrubs and palms; a stream poured loudly down past us to the relic-less plains; birds whistled and hooted. The mountain had served as an irresistible landmark for the old Indian traders. But ancient Katha had left nothing behind. Except a hundred or so more temple bases for archaeologists to probe. And a superb, stone nine-inch-high standing Buddha, which Kamaruddin keeps locked up in a filing cabinet.

Kamaruddin had a final word. "Remember, Thais came into the north of Malaya; Achinese people lower down; Bugis sea-rovers moved into Selangor; Minangkabau people from west Sumatra into Negri Sembilan; Bugis again in Malacca and Johor," he said, seeing me off with a cheery wave of the hand and a rippling laugh. "What a mix-up!" But before heading south, I retraced my steps to the capital of the oldest Sultanate, Kedah. Alor Star: the beautiful name may sound like a serene and distant planet, but it has its feet very much muddied in solid agricultural earth. Your plane will land in what looks like, and is, an immense emerald padi field, intersected by canals as straight as lines on a graph paper. In its midst a chunk of rock pokes up through the greenness like a huge and improbable brownish wedge of cheese partly nibbled by giant prehistoric rats.

Alor Star's central square is superb: a great mosque, all domes and fine minarets, dominates it, faced and flanked by the Sultan's Balai Besar, a ceremonial hall, and the best of two museums, full of old photographs, one of which in particular spans much history: at a 1927 dinner of the Malay Society in London you see two men whose lives straddle the last momentous hundred years of Malaysia: the young Tunku Abdul Rahman, Malaysia's first Prime Minister and Grand Old Man (buried in 1990 at Langgi nearby) and the ageing Sir Frank Swettenham, one of the most gifted and swashbuckling of Britain's old colonial servants in Malaya.

Turn your back on the modern fountain — the best thing to do to it — and you see the Balai Nobat where the royal orchestra plays on restricted occasions; an affair mainly of drums and brass gongs whose morose and antique sounds echoing from the past tend to strike a superstitious dread in all young Malays who hear it.

It was by a stroke of luck that I caught sight of the motorcyclist with a pigtailed macaque on his pillion. The monkey looked me full in the eye as it passed me, and I lengthened my stride to follow it. Otherwise I would have missed the café and temple behind China Street on the river where old ferry boatmen rowed passengers standing up, chewing their cheap cigars, their amulets swaying round their neck. It was a memorable scene. The café's terrace lay on a bend so that the beautiful milk-white mosque in its hedge of trees faced it, reflected exactly in the

Dominic Sansoni

Steve McCurry

water like an illustration in 1001 Nights. I drink fresh limejuice, the healthiest drink in the tropics, at a terrace table among a number of Indians and Chinese while, as the sun died in an oyster sky, the ceramic dragons on the temple roof frenziedly twisted their limbs, and one even stood on its head. Soon, from that extraordinary mosque a soft baritone call to prayer drifted to us across the water. If I never go back there, I shall always remember Alor Star for that enchanted moment.

Waiting for the Langkawi Express Mr Balakrishnan, the stationmaster at Alor Star, stalks up the platform to make sure the signals are set correctly. Tall, straight-backed as a regimental sergeant-major, in white uniform and black songkok, he strokes his fierce moustache and contemplates the 15 signal levers with labels on them saying things like "Point Down Main Line Loop" and "Shunt to Main". "All in order," he assures me.

"No steam, sir. All diesel," he goes on. Then he juggles with a communications system of heavy metal and brass keys that look as if they have been there since Frank Swettenham became Resident of Selangor. The whole archaic contraption is marked "Tyer and Company Ltd, Signalling Engineers, Reading". "This is coming from your place," Mr Balakrishnan explains. Soon the Express rattles in and jolts to a stop. I find my seat in an airconditioned carriage with a television set. It has comfortable seats that lean back. An unwatchable horror film full of blood and carnage is being shown, and a middle-aged man is watching it with his small son, their eyes goggling.

As we begin to move I shout to Mr Balakrishnan in mock

Rubber tappers start work before dawn, to avoid daytime heat. Another way to keep cool in Malaysia is to drink freshly-squeezed lime juice.

anxiety, "Signals set okay?" "Naturally, sir," he shouts back cheerfully waving his green flag. "We can't have you going off the rails." And, equally cheerfully, "Malaysian National Railways wish you all the best," cried the Indian guard whose grandfather he has told me was born in Trichinopoly — "Trichy," he called it, as if we were both old India hands.

All the best is, in the event, what we got. Curry and rice and fine scenery. With something extra, for between Kuala Kangsar, which is the royal city of Perak State, and my destination at Ipoh, the old tin-mining centre, we plunged into jungle as into a tunnel. The trees closed in; leaves brushed the windows; we seemed to rattle down the streets of kampongs; small butterflies flew in and out. If a macaque had dropped in on the end of a creeper, like Tarzan, it would not have been surprising. We reached Ipoh on time, and I was sorry to have to disembark.

Nomachi

Uncontrolled feudalism in the Malay States began to give way to bureaucracy when the Malay College (now open to any talented Malay, not necessarily royalty) was set up in 1904. A handsome academic facade faces wide playing-fields and the Clifford English School whose motto is written in large letters on a gatepost: "The Ship is worth more than the Crew" — a dubious 19th-century maxim that takes me back to the adventurous novels of Captain Marryat and Robert Louis Stevenson. It would have appealed, though, to the whiskered British officials you can inspect in a magnificent collection of old photographs of former Sultans and their advisers. There they sit, looking haughtily off-camera; some seem embarrassingly aware that they are better qualified for the cricket field than for handling tricky affairs of state in Malaya; others, one would quite like to meet, look like EM Forster.

In Ipoh you are in another world: a Chinese world, at that. Its chequerboard streets are emblazoned with Chinese notice boards; loud guttural barks of Hokkien or Cantonese explode around you like crackers at Chinese New Year. Only the ancient FMS bar, filled no doubt by the invisible ghosts of countless planters and tin-miners, caters for Indians with Tiger Beer and eggs, bacon and chips, while the secondary school across the padang displays a facade less befitting Ipoh than a film production of *Tom Brown's Schooldays*.

Many rich Chinese families come out from Ipoh at weekends in their Nissans and Hondas to gaze at the huge limestone walls of the Perak Cave Shrine, dominated by impressive wall paintings of Buddhas in swirling robes and faces, haloed with hair, that have un-Oriental hooked noses strangely like Mr Punch. A donations box near an immense golden Buddha rumbled like a bass drum when I dropped a small coin into it. Soon a large group of garrulous Chinese sightseers strolled up to the image. They stared and moved on, still chattering — the donations box made no sound.

The influence of the Malay College in replacing feudalism with bureaucracy was limited. After all, there are still nine rulers — one of whom is chosen by his peers as King of Malaysia every five years. But the once unfettered rulers now play a largely ceremonial role in accord with the federal constitution. An elected Federal Government in Kuala Lumpur, of course, governs the country — *Tria juncta in uno.* Within the states, leaders are elected to state assemblies which manage the state's day-to-day affairs. Each ruler has a ceremonial role in state affairs, and is head of his state religion (Islam, of course).

I went to call on one of the most responsible and beneficent rulers. He owns a superb old palace of wood of west Sumatran design — no nails were used in its construction — next to a mini-Buckingham Palace of dubious aesthetic value where he holds investitures and receptions. The custom for a ruler to be personally available to the most humble of people persists, I was glad to be told. A handsome 67-year-old in pink slacks, a sports shirt and suede slippers, the ruler said: "Oh, yes. People continually come to see me with problems. Perhaps, for example, someone feels the government has unjustly taken his land. Perhaps he has some marital tangle. Perhaps it has to do with inheritance. We sort it out. Or try to."

Basil Pao

Dominic Sansoni

There has been some mild controversy about whether Malay princes should involve themselves in business activities. It has been pointed out that the British Royal Family does not deal in stocks and shares. Yet the two sons of the ruler I have mentioned are extraordinarily successful businessmen. No one criticizes them. The two Tunkus — who were educated at an English public school, like some other Malaysian "royals" — have now started up a school for Malaysian boys and girls which will provide cheaply the same high standard of education Malays once had to pay through the nose for in England. This surely is patriotic endeavour.

Nor is that all. The younger of these patriotic Tunkus is also a motivating force in the Heritage organisation — an unofficial group trying to restore buildings of historic or aesthetic value that

are on the point of crumbling away — a cultural disaster that particularly threatens all the elaborate 19th-century Chinese houses, temples, and shops of Penang and the barely surviving magnificence of Baba and Nonya (Straits Chinese) Malacca.

Preserving old houses is a costly business. These days it takes more than royalty. It is time others joined in. Malacca is small and jewel-like; a quiet port guarded by an old fort and the Dutch Town Hall at the end of a long highway from Johor and Kuala Lumpur, that pushes through the industrial sprawl of Selangor, then plunges — in relief — through slender rubber trees and rows of newly-planted palm-oil trees, like big pineapple tops. Isabella Bird, travelling bravely here in 1879, likened Malacca to "Sleepy Hollow" and remarked to bearded Mr Briggs, the chaplain who ferried her ashore to a deserted jetty, that it seemed to her to be "out of the running". Pestered by the biggest mosquitoes she had ever seen, intrepid old "Birdie", travelling by elephant at three miles an hour, was soon fed up with that mode of transport. The elephant kept squirting muddy water at her, and when she whacked him with her umbrella "he uttered the loudest roar I have ever heard".

The Bird's Eye view of Malacca (however "out of the running" it may have seemed) would have included some very grand houses indeed and the great hill — Bukit Cina — which countless Chinese immigrant notables (mostly from Fujian Province) had scattered with graves as big as miniature amphitheatres. Perhaps we need Isabella Bird now to take her umbrella to some of the Chinese billionaire sons of Malacca who

Chinese nuns in the Buddhist Cheng Hoon Teng — Temple of Pure Clouds — practise the art of calligraphy when not chanting or meditating.

left to make their fortunes in Singapore and elsewhere; men who could easily afford to help with the urgently needed restoration of their birthplace and insist on a halt to the destruction of the old harbour — where in 1405, Admiral Cheng Ho, commander of the Imperial Ming fleet anchored 50 junks-of-war — by ham-fisted reclamation. If Malacca-born Chinese businessmen, thoughtful of their roots and mindful of their conscience, do not come forward Malacca (and Penang) will be "out of the running" for good and "Sleepy Hollow" will be enveloped in the Sleep of Death.

Like Renaissance Italian princes, Malaysian royalty has for centuries been patron to the traditional Malay arts, providing money and royal premises in which, for instance, expensively costumed dance-dramas like the *menora* and *makyung* can be performed to live orchestras. All this in the courts of Kelantan and Trengganu, above all. In Trengganu and Kelantan another art survives — flourishes, rather — thanks to royalty. There is the making of songket: unbelievably beautiful,

fine gold and silver-threaded sarongs, and even wedding suits for royal bridegrooms or any Malay who wants to look like, as they say, "a king for the day". A young Malay bridegroom dressed from head to foot in yellow and gold could be mistaken for a sun-god in a reception room which a hundred male guests in Trengganu songkets have turned into a hall of rainbows.

Clifford said: "The Trengganu Malay excels as an artisan, at woodcarving, brass." This is true today, though to emphasise royal involvement in these traditions, Kelantan boldly claims the

finest songkets. It is a moot point. One of the best small weaving houses is in the house of a most subtle designer, a nephew of the ruler of Trengganu called Tengku Ismail. One of his girl weavers, sitting in a window rolling gold thread onto a spindle, reminded me of a princess in a story by Grimm imprisoned in a turret, spinning her own blonde hair into a rope up which her lover would climb to set her free. More beautiful even than Thai silk, songket will not die out. Kite flying, too, I suspect, will survive. Kites soar into the sky from every village street, and popular competitions are numerous.

The same cannot be said of ancient dance-dramas of North Malaysia. Or the playing of ancient Malay instruments, like the three stringed *rebab*. Both are on the verge of extinction. I flew across the Peninsula, across dark bumps of mountain and jungle, separated by cloud layers like whipped cream, and then travelled by car to a remote kampong in Trengganu specifically to flush out one of the last rebab performers, an oldish man called Idris.

I found him at last, sitting on the steps of a stilted house in a landscape of flat shimmering green. With his ample wife, a well-known dancer of *makyung* herself, he was lunching off a breadfruit which they asked me to share.

It was a bitter-sweet encounter. It was sweet to hear the melancholy sounds Idris drew from his gaily-painted instrument, holding it upright like a miniature cello and drawing across it a bow of surprisingly slack coconut-fibre strings; it was bitter to hear him sadly admit that although local people loved (crowded in, in fact) to hear him play, the young of the kampongs had no interest in learning to do so. They preferred — need I say it? — electric guitars.

Traditional bridal attire is very ornate in Malacca, whether the bride is Malay or a Straits Chinese nonya. The beaded and filigreed headdress of this Malay bride could well complement the nonya's beaded slippers, reflecting cultural cross currents here.

The best way to sight Kuching and its river — probably one of the most unobtrusively exciting views in the world — is from a ship. I saw it the first time on the eve of Chinese New Year arriving from Singapore under the great shaggy sentinel of Santubong Mountain at sunset. Before us the sunset cast tongues of blood on the river that twisted its way to the former capital of the White Rajahs through mangrove and creepered trees, while behind it wave after wave of mountain and forest rose up and faded in a purple haze into the black Borneo night.

Kong hee fat choy! the Chinese crew shouted ecstatically to each other as the sun went down behind the distant black fist of Tanjung Datu behind which lies Kalimantan. "Happy New Year!" they cried, and their happy faces matched the fiery colour of the sunset as the brandy took effect.

I remember the lights of pressure-lamps shining from the doll's house doorways of tiny stilted houses clinging to the river banks, showing in their shadowy interiors a few dark-skinned men in sarongs crouched round low fires. Further up where the first lights of the town appeared there were barges and small boats moored alongside low warehouses at a bend in the river. Across the water, the old Astana of the Rajahs gleamed on its green slope like a ghostly relic of a hundred or more years ago. Of all the towns of the east it is rational to claim Kuching as the most atmospheric. It is small, about the size of an English market town. It was never bombed as most towns of Borneo and Indonesia were in the Second World War. Its dull-gold domed mosque and low, sedate buildings have been there long enough to give one a very good idea of what Kuching has been like since the early days of James Brooke — those fierce days of regular raids, murder, pillage and slave-taking, of heroes and villains of several colours and races.

How can one forget Conrad's old Sulu pirate, Babalatchi — the one-eyed statesman, crocodile, factotum, harbour master, prime minister to the Rajah of Sambir — in *Almayer's Folly* and

An Outcast of the Islands? "Some of the pirates were very fine men, brave, fierce," said Conrad, "never giving quarter to Europeans." And Babalatchi, talking to an English seaman, regretted the days of glory up the coast of Sarawak from Kuching to Brunei — his days as a true Orang Laut, Man of the Sea: *"Ah, Tuan!...the old days were the best. Even I have boarded at night silent ships with white sails. That was before an English Rajah ruled in Kuching. Then we fought among ourselves and were happy. Now when we fight with you we can only die...."*

Piracy was never a pastime of the indigenous people of West Borneo, though their coast from June to July was annually infested by the sea-rovers from the Sulu Archipelago between Sabah and the Philippine island of Mindanao. Their fleets regularly roamed the mouth of the Sarawak River and the small island of Satang. Now the clash of krises has gone forever and the roar of cannon exists only in the thunder. You lie back in your yacht, or throw a line over the side and close your eyes. The chestnut-backed Brahminy kite (magical to the Dayaks) swoops lazily down over the nipah palms. Earth, sky and the romantic river-mouth lie about you as if in a deep sleep.

Kuching has priceless advantages; it is beautiful; it is built on a human scale and has a romantic past. Above all, a good many Ibans live there, which makes it an extremely warmhearted place. It also shares with Peninsular Malaysia something of extreme importance — a mixed and magnificent cuisine, Chinese, Malay and Indian. It must be said that one of Malaysia's principal blessings is that you can eat as good a meal as you have ever had for less than 50p sterling or a good bit less than one US dollar. An old British-Malaysian friend of mine, 'Bushy' Webb, who has lived in Sarawak for many years, takes me to eat a mouth-flaying curry off a banana leaf, but you don't pay more if you want to eat it off a plate.

That first time, Kuching was not at its quietest; the crackers of Chinese New Year had just begun exploding. They had exciting names and I made a list of some of them: *Ground*

Bloom Flowers, Sparkling Wheel, Peacock Fountain, Silvery Glitter Flower, King Cat Sparklers, Moon Flitting Phoenix, and *Electric Sparks.* They made an amazing din. Coupled with the Chinese boys roaring by in trucks, joyfully banging drums and clashing cymbals, it sounded as if a war had broken out.

Kuching has always looked to me very much like an engraving from a 19th-century book of travel in Sarawak. Now I heard a disquieting rumour about the little town. Tourist group leaders from Singapore, the story went, had declared quite forcefully that they were deeply bored by history, old buildings, Dayak longhouses or relics of bygone rajahs. Their plan for a new Kuching was to pull the old waterside buildings down and build big, towering shopping centres instead. Of course, that would kill Kuching and serious tourism at one stroke.

On this visit, shrugging such a nightmare vision aside, I planned to go to Sibu and by boat up the Rajang River, the longest river in Sarawak, one which virtually cuts the state in half so that British troops nicknamed it the M1 after Britain's main north-south highway. The Dayaks lived along its banks and I wanted to see a longhouse.

"In the days of the Rajah," said 'Bushy', recalling pre-independence days, "I lived at Sibu. It was nothing much then. The Island Club had 30 or 40 members. Just a wooden bungalow, a tennis court and a bowling alley. But most evenings we gathered there: the Resident, the district officer, the police superintendent, the land-survey-wallah, the public works engineer, a judge, a doctor, and people like me. I was in timber then."

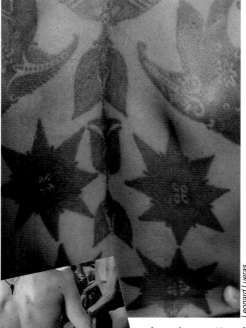

Leonard Lueras

Dennis Lau

Now, as I soon found when my plane landed there, Sibu has changed. There are big ships in the port and the spreading suburbs of expensive houses reach out to the airport belonging to Chinese who have made their pile in logging. Logging is the big business here, as the oil industry is further on in Miri and Bintulu.

With Melintan, my Iban guide from Kuching, I reached the town called Kapit at the 'heart' of the Rajang. In one of the express-boats that dash regularly up the river in a cloud of spray, hoping to avoid the enormous logs floating down in the opposite direction, we made it in three hours. Kapit is a tiny place in a green and well-tended area — a small market town for the Ibans who farm in the region. Kapit's mayor, an Iban educated in Nashville, Tennessee, presides with great verve over a very large and sprawling area of Sarawak which is mostly forest, water, and patches of straightforward agriculture. Iban affairs are in the hands of Ibans.

The river is, in truth, the highway. Everybody and everything upriver depends on it. Huge log-rafts are towed down it to the sea by tug from the logging camps high up the Rajang; goods and passengers speed up it as high as they can in the other direction; and Ibans from distant longhouses bring goods to Kapit market in canoes propelled by outboard motors. The Ibans struck me immediately as the most charming, gentle people I had ever met — an impression which, reinforced day by day, culminated in a visit to an Iban longhouse very far even from Kapit.

Ibans, sometimes known as Sea Dayaks, are the majority race of Dayaks; people say there are 400,000 of them. They live in longhouses, and many also work in government offices in Kapit, Sibu and Kuching, or on the oilfields or in timber-felling camps. Like Malays in the

Heavy tattoos were traditional for older Iban men but many in the younger generation disdain this symbol of masculinity which, in any event, would now be hidden by their Western attire of T-shirts and jeans.

Peninsula, who hurry to their kampongs at Hari Raya, Ibans at every opportunity head back to their natal longhouses. Some Ibans are Christians, some not. The Bidayuhs (Land Dayaks) are mostly Christians; and another race, the Melanaus, are both Muslim and Christian. High up in the remotest forest clearings live other races — the *Orang Ulu* (men of the forest), some nomadic. To find some of these shyest of people is often like searching for fleas in a mat; they are, to say the least, elusive. The nomadic Penans, the Punans, Kayans, Kenyahs dwell obscurely in the region of Brunei, the Baram River and Mount Mulu, numbering some 70,000 people.

What one must accept at once, and however regretfully, is that the days of the naked long-haired Dayak warrior, clad only in a loincloth and complicated tattoos — Noble Savages with blowpipes — is gone. This is the time of baseball caps and shorts or jeans. Thank heavens what remains is the Dayaks' love of their longhouse life, their magic and their birds.

A longboat with a roaring outboard motor bore Melintan and myself up the river at speed. The water is either high or low — a mark on a house in Kapit shows that on one unforgettable occasion the waters of the Rajang rose sixty feet. If it is very high, the river ahead may look like a very choppy sea. The water rushes down with frightening force over enormous rocks hidden, but only just, by the frothing, swirling deluge. An expert boatman is essential. You could hit rocks, be overturned by turbulent waves which come at you from all sides, lose your engine, your headway and all control in the maelstrom; people are drowned here every year. These rapids are no joking matter. At the Pelagus Rapids on the way to Belaga, the disembowelled wreck of an express-boat stands on a rock like a terrible warning.

When the water is low (say, August, September) you will have to get out and wade, only ankle-deep, pushing your heavy boat over four-foot boulders. Melintan had had that particular experience. But in this season of exceptional rains he

and I were now swept by the erratic (but expert) steering of our boatman from one side of the river to the other to miss those fiendish rocks.

We pulled into the shore in a narrow tributary of the Rajang after five hours of travel. The approach to the longhouse was far above us, a steep slippery climb up rotting wooden steps embedded in mud. A longhouse is basically what it says: a long, wooden house on stilts with a wide verandah with a crumbling plank floor so apparently feeble that I felt I was bound to fall through it into the mud beneath. Behind that a series of twenty-four plywood 'doors' each concealing a room or two in which one family lives, sleeps and cooks. I had read that longhouse walls were often covered with pictures of the Queen of England. In this one, only pretty, blank-faced Malay pop stars looked complacently down on us brandishing guitars.

On the verandah everything happens except sleep. People sit and talk, roll damp cigarettes in palm leaves, pour tea; feed children; fend off dogs, snorting pigs and tall, long-legged fighting cocks. Beneath the see-through floor of rotting, mildewed slats, more pigs rootle and the smoke from unseen fires trickles up to disperse mosquitoes. Despite the noise, the Ibans are quiet, deliberate people. You take at once to such gentle human beings with such kind eyes.

Dinner with our host, the longhouse headman, was corned beef, green vegetable, yams, rice. When the older men were gathered later, we drank tuak rice wine, from a tin kettle. It went down a treat; smooth, cool, refreshing, inspiring one old man to burble on proudly of his adventures with British forces in Malaya in the 1950s, employed as a 'tracker' to sniff out Communist guerrillas. He was young then, had long hair, wore a loincloth, and had come to like whisky in the sergeants' mess, he said with a smile, so I gave him a cupful to remind him of old times.

There were no hornbill feathers or loincloths. Hornbill country was faraway to the northeast. The old men — and our host — were heavily tattooed, but they dance only at festivals.

I asked a young man back from an oil-town about that. He said, smiling, "My father takes that seriously. I don't." He didn't think that much about tattoos, adding, "Well, it hurts." Everyone laughed. We didn't need any dancing. Things were quite lively enough as it was.

Iban hospitality overcomes one. Tribal Arabs are hospitable, but even they can't compare with this. You give Ibans a few shamefully insignificant gifts — sweets for children, cigarettes. You eat three meals a day; and repeat each meal in perhaps seven or eight other 'doors' of the same longhouse. It's the same with the tuak. A few cups with one family, more with another, and another, and so on. You need a hard head. Everyone staggers after a while. Luckily, Ibans don't resent tipsiness; they only resent a flat refusal to drink. To be polite you need an excuse. Even a feeble "Sorry, doctor's orders" will do.

It is easy to see how the longhouse life would grow on one, and why the longhouse children come back to it. Loneliness is unknown there, for one thing. A longhouse, after all, is an extended family crammed under one roof. Everyone shares; everyone is protected; everyone is equal. How could one live in a silent, lonely flat after the comforting din of a longhouse? Once accustomed to it, you would miss the maddening but somehow reassuring noise at daybreak.

First of all comes pigs feeding-time. The women en masse call them in with a deafening hallooing: "Hoo-ooo-ey!" This sets off a cacophony of several dozen roosters; followed by two or

three packs of dogs; then the babies. By five o'clock the racket is so appalling that you stagger from your mattress down to the river to wash, praying for someone to offer you a quiet mug of tea. When, after a period of polite watchfulness, Iban eyes — intensely shy at first — stop flicking warily back and forth, they are ready to take their cue from the visitor's mood. Strong-willed women drag you from room to room offering you rice and fish and palm shoots, coffee or tea. You are taken to bath in a creek nearby where the muddy river's floodwater does not try to sweep you down to Sibu, but fresh rivulets form deep clear rock pools under the shadows of huge trees.

Of course, education has killed off many Iban traditions. Head-hunting, the government has taught people, is 'not quite the thing' — and in any case was ever only approved of when there was a war and the heads were adult, male and hostile. A mild magic, though, persists. One night I spotted one of the older men with unbelievably thin joints, wrinkled skin and a network of large veins over arms and hands, draw a sharp dagger across the stomach of a baby. A human sacrifice? No, the old man was a shaman, and the knife was part of a ritual to cure the baby's colic. Up the river, an old outboard motor was propped up in a graveyard to insure a departed one's transfer to the spirit world at a reasonable 20 knots.

Having no written traditions, Ibans make up for it with songs. There are songs for every eventuality. A song of a woman looking for a love-charm. (A love-charm, in case you need it, can be made of flowers and oil mixed with the tears of the rare dugong, a snub-nosed sea mammal once called the Queen of the Fish.) Most Iban songs refer prettily to the birds and flora they live with. A lullaby,

Leonard Lueras

Michael Freeman

The *pedam*, the traditional Iban sword, formerly used by head-hunters to secure their trophies. Although the practice of head-hunting has stopped since World War II, many longhouses still display the trophies of their forefathers.

for instance, begins: *The night bird calls / heavy with sobs, it weeps for a nesting-place / where it may sleep.* The poor nightbird (the Hawk owl) endlessly searches for his former wife, the Moon, who has abandoned him on earth. On extra dark nights you hear him calling and calling. Then spirit mediums have a number of songs. And one I like about Iban girls returning from bathing describes them walking quickly and wisely like the empitu bird (the Painted Quail).

In these songs the girls are always attractive, wise and capable; sometimes tough, and even warlike like the hermaphroditic Fireback Pheasant. The young men are bachelors, handsome naturally, and spoiled, Hornbill-like, hot-blooded, and to my mind a little idiotic. They hide their feelings "but of course they surge within".

The immemorial Iban courting process is odd. The bachelor visits an unmarried girl under her mosquito-net at night when summoned by sweet blasts on her mouth-harp. Perched on her bedside, he talks to her softly within earshot of her parents: nothing more. If she permits it he can return for a second chat. A third probably leads to betrothal. If she finds him gauche or boring she is at liberty to chuck him out of her loft. In one amusing song about this practice, a mother merrily questions her son about certain bruises he sustained, according to him, by tripping over a log. A likely story, she thinks. In fact he has been hurled unceremoniously from a girl's loft. "Get off the planks of my bed..." she fumes. And "the lovely impulsive young girl" suddenly pushes him "by the neck so he falls all the way from the top to the bottom...his vision blurring like the eyes of a cock at evening." "It was nothing, mother," he says. "Don't worry, I merely sprained my left hand and dislocated my lower right jaw." Poor boy! For him it is, as Dayaks don't say, back to square one.

Returning to Kapit, we embark for another five hours through rough water and thick jungle. Beautiful Rajah Brooke birdwing butterflies hover over the pig-pen in a quivering cloud — black or purple, with green patterns on six-inch wings and scarlet heads. Then as the boat pulls away, the jungle closes in. Jungle, you thought, was just jungle. Now you see how varied it is. Nipah palms explode in a cluster like a frozen bomb burst. A sudden bronze, absolutely smooth trunk stands like a naked human torso sixty foot high. Some tracks of jungle are dark and sombre, others pale almost yellow, or grey with a rusty tinge; trees like silver tubes soar upwards, and a sudden flattened patch of undergrowth looks as if a brontosaurus has stepped there.

Now and again, of course, the trees have been ripped away, and bare earth is all there is, and the noise of mechanical grabs clambering about barren red sandhills. Can we say, paraphrasing Kipling, "Out of the spent and unconsidered earth, the forests will rise again"?

Who knows? What we can hear if we have ears to hear, is an Iban voice, rising sad and sweet over the roar and crash of the water, over the calls of strange birds, over the wonderful silence enveloping trees and hillsides as old as time: *Wo-o-o-o-o-o...Mercy be for the poor passionate girls, hearts aroused, stirred to search for lovers they have not got, for the beloved one who will stay always. Aye-o-o-o-....*

Dominic Sansoni

Dominic Sansoni

Urban development in Malaysia has not eliminated traditional housing styles but the *Peranakan* architectural trimmings which used to be found all over Malacca and Penang are now in danger of being sold off to antique shops in Singapore.

At Kota Kinabalu I was a few days nearer Chinese New Year than I had been in Kuching, and the fireworks on sale had increased in number and beautified their names into the bargain — *Baby Mouse Blooms, Butterflies Welcoming Spring, Little Bird, Dancing Fresh Flowers, Successive Happy News.* I hadn't been to Sabah for 10 years, and it had been Chinese New Year then, too: the Year of the Monkey had been approaching. The city of Kota Kinabalu had not much impressed me then. I was concentrating every effort on finding an illegal launch to carry me from Sandakan to the Filipino port of Mindanao through a pirate-infested sea. It wasn't a sea that was simply thought to be infested with pirates — there was no doubt that it really was. Newspapers reported hijackings at sea, almost daily. It always has been like this. From time immemorial, sea-rovers had annually sortied out from their havens in the Sulu Islands to raid the coastal settlements of North Borneo (Sabah) and Kalimantan, taking slaves as they went. Those days, operating in slim, outriggers or boats with outboard engines and heavy machine-guns they attacked quite large cargo ships. It had become their way of life years ago; for them a good way.

We were all very rich then — ah! such numbers of beautiful wives, and such feasting! — but above all, we had a great many holy men in our force! — such brass guns, such long pendants, such krises, fighting cocks, such smoking opium, and eating white rice.

That was the view of one Sulu rover of 200 years ago. Now, without the preoccupation of a voyage round the world, I could take another look at Kota Kinabalu. And I found it was truly beautiful. I hadn't remembered a sea so clear and green or islands so peaceful and serene. I had been concentrating on pirates too much to see that!

Nor had I taken such a close look at the great Magic Mountain itself. Mount Kinabalu is big, over 13,000 feet — but somehow seems much bigger: almost as big as some monster of the Himalayas. I think it must be something to do with the clouds

and its own odd shape. You peer at the first layer of thick cloud, quite high up, and you see part of a ridge, dark and impressive. That's the peak, you say to yourself. And soon you realise in amazement that there is another, much larger shelf of rock emerging much higher up from the very top of the cloud. That is the true peak. It is relatively flat, but rather jagged too. Like a black cock's comb.

The effect is one of awesome beauty, but with a tinge of menace. There is an air of Valhalla, of a place where gods might live. No wonder the Dusuns think it prudent to offer on occasion some trifling offering. One British Governor of North Borneo neglected to do so, and for some time guests met him on the residency stairs long after his rather sudden death.

The National Park round the lower slopes of the mountain have no such hauntings, but is a sanctuary for Sabah's extraordinary birds. All you must do is to stand on some exposed knoll in the trees and wait for their sounds — seldom their sight — to reach you. One — a green barbet — goes *O-tock...o-tock...o-tock* until you want to urge it to stop. One sounds like a man chopping a log. The lonely call of the treepie, a bird with a long, ungainly tail, is designed to bring friends around, said my guide smiling — "No Sabahan likes to be alone for long." The bird I liked best, so small I never could see it, made a tweedly noise like those odd devices that unlock your car doors at fifty paces.

Over on the northeast coast near Sandakan, across the bay beyond the miniature rock of Gibraltar that guards its entrance, you plunge into a very mysterious watery world — part salt, part fresh — where it is not difficult to get lost in a maze of the identical waterways of a much dispersed delta. Here white-collared fish eagles scout the tangle of islands; Brahminy kites soar overhead on wing feathers spread like supple fingers on a dancer's hand; and white egrets stand motionless as marble statues among the mangroves.

I had only seen proboscis monkeys, stuffed, in the

Kuching museum — outrageous creatures with bulbous noses like heavy-drinking Europeans, and actually called *Orang Belanda* (Dutchmen) by Ibans, perhaps to show what they thought of the colonisers of Kalimantan. I thought I recognised one or two friends.

On the river I speak of, the proboscis monkeys take life — the riverside trees are agitated by the big chestnut-brown bodies, those embarrassing noses point dubiously down at you, the long tails dangle straight down like bell-ropes of grey plush.

As much at home in these backwaters, the Bajaus have built their ever-expanding water kampongs far out over the crab-infested mudflats. The Bajaus are scattered all over the Malay Peninsula. I have come across them far away in the Gulf of Bone in Bugis territory. Their origins are mysterious. They are the Sea-gypsies — the *orang laut* — and have nothing to do with piracy: fishing and minor trading is their metier.

At Sepilok orangutan sanctuary, who was most happy — the orangutans or the tourists who thought the feeding show had been called off due to heavy rain, but found it was on? The question changed and became: will Raja and Donny behave like gentlemen today? From time to time they have been lecherously attracted to tourists showing off bra-less nipples and tried to pinch them. Only high spirits, say their keepers.

This time they behaved as if they'd been well brought up as feminists all their lives. We stood under tall trees whose foliage was battered by falling rain and springing hairy red-limbed monkeys who seemed to be all legs and arms. They threw down leaves and small twigs impatiently from time to time to urge their keepers to hurry up with their bananas and pails of milk. And when the keepers hurried up shouting: "Hey! Raja! Hey, Donny!" the two oldest orangutans responded, stretching down long shaggy arms to receive their rations. (Donny is named, I believe, after a famous Mormon pop-singer called Donny Osmond, but any resemblance must be coincidental).

Tribes of macaques, pigtailed and red-behinded like baboons, were the comic villains of the show. Like Kipling's bandarlog, they sprang about, raiding outrageously any bananas they could filch from the very mouths of the good-natured and slower orangutans. But everyone got enough in the end and most of the goings-on were filmed. Leaving the sanctuary, I looked up to see two pied hornbills, far away on the bare top of a tree, grotesque silhouettes against the stormy sky, skeletons with wings.

I am sure the best way to see the uplands — if you haven't got the flora and fauna expert called David de la Harpe to drive you as I had — is by the tiny rattling train that leaves Beaufort and ploughs its gentle, unsophisticated way over the Crocker Range to Tenom. Or come back by the train from Tenom to Beaufort. People said it was only worth doing once. I disagree. It is not the comfort of a toy train that appeals, but being on a toy train at all. The local people on it, from the villages, up the hillsides, cram aboard, chattering and laughing; you can get out at the miniscule stations and walk about; old women bring things to eat. It is a very simple pleasure. And at the end of it is the Lagud Sembrang orchid centre, two acres of orchid-draped trees, a stream, and beautiful blooms. About 10 percent of all the world's orchids are in Borneo — the hybridisation process goes on continually. To Tony Lamb, the orchid specialist who runs the centre, I said, "If I asked you to 'mix me' an orchid, say, pink and peach in colour with — or, let's see — scarlet stripes in it, could you?" "Yes," he said at once. "And as a matter of fact there is one just like that."

Walking through sealing-wax palms and Norfolk pines, admiring white and yellow Moon orchids, he said: "The more you go into wild orchids, the more you like the smaller ones." I looked at a clump of what looked like ferns on a branch, surely not an orchid. But it was. An orchid can look like practically anything, even an arrangement of seven-foot hanging leaves you take for broad beans if you don't look too closely, can be an orchid. The smallest orchids were about the size of a very, very intricately-coloured midge.

A significant thing happened just before I left Kota Kinabalu. I decided to visit one of the many karaoke joints, which have sprung up all over Asia. Here, in a disco atmosphere, men and women — presumably with considerable egos — stand up in public and sing standard pop numbers, supported by a recorded background of music and video films which illustrate on a screen what the song is about. For instance, to a good many off-key renderings of I Left My Heart in San Francisco we were shown a background of the Golden Gate with the setting sun behind it.

Enough is enough, and I was rising to leave when the unlikely thing happened. A young Dusun edged nervously to the podium and began to sing. The song, in Dusun, was about a village market in Sabah; about the fruits and vegetables on sale there. Pineapples, cabbages, sweet potatoes, and so on also appeared on the film. I thought: there is a man who loves his home. He didn't want to imitate Sinatra singing My Way; exiled from the village he loved, he wanted to sing about that. I very much doubt if I shall ever enter a karaoke place again. But I shall never forget that Dusun and his song of home.

Dominic Sansoni

So where was this spirit, or soul, of Malaysia I had been seeking? I hadn't been everywhere by a long chalk. But I think I have been to enough places to know at least where that spirit does not reside. It does not reside, for example, in the muddle and industrial slum of modern Selangor. It is not crouched there somewhere among the factories, the highways, the traffic jams and the hideous cheap housing. Nor, I am willing to bet, was it making itself at home in the bunkers and greens of the accelerating number of golf courses by which Southeast Asian tourists, in particular, are being lured to Malaysia. Nor can it possibly be housed in the towering monstrosity of Penang's Komtar tower, a shopping-centre it is easier to get lost in than anywhere since the Minotaur's maze at Knossos. No, it was not there; never had been, never would be.

I have some idea where it is to be discovered. In the kampongs, as I said; and in the old houses of Malacca and Penang. I am certain it is hovering very happily under Mount Kedah where Kamaruddin tends his ancient temples among whistling birds and rushing waterfalls. The young Dusun singing a love-song to his village, knows it. Mr Idris, the old rebab player who shared his breadfruit with me, lives with it every minute of the day; so does the girl weaving golden songket in Tengku Ismail's factory, the one who reminded me of a Grimm's fairy princess in an abandoned turret. Everyone knows it lurks on the clouded crown of Mount Kinabalu. It flaps on the wings of the Rhinoceros Hornbill through the forests of Sarawak and is heard in the song Ibans sing, almost in the language of Coleridge, of an eloping couple "going speedily as the blowpipe dart made of tekalong wood, arriving at the wide flat plain, the place where the poisonous Moon Cobra watches the track where everyone goes back and forth." Under Santubong, the great sentinel mountain of Kuching, the local people see it in the upper ridges which delineate, they say, the outline of the White Rajah looking up to heaven.

In all these places, the spirit of Malaysia is alive and well, and watching. In places like these you find, as Hugh Clifford once did, that the moon is waiting to fall into your lap.

Evidence of Malaysia's racial tolerance is everywhere — young Muslim women with their heads covered in the prevailing Islamic fashion can be seen in areas displaying Chinese cultural patterns.

Many of the mostly Malay villagers living on the east coast fish, or combine vegetable and rice farming with fishing and low-level entrepreneurship. Women in the northernmost east coast state of Kelantan are well-known for their independent spirit and entrepreneurial ability. In fishing villages like tiny Pantai Subak, the women sell the fish caught by their menfolk. Women also take most of the responsibility for processing the surplus catch, cleaning, salting and drying the fish on bamboo racks. Salted fish is a low cost addition to the diet, and it is popular in Malay and Chinese cooking.

The men in the fishing villages on Peninsular Malaysia's east coast were described in 1911 by British historian Richard Winstedt thus: "They were once pirates to a man and in the later days, they were a rough, hard-bit gang, ignorant and superstitious beyond belief, tanned to the colour of mahogany by exposure to the sun, with faces scarred by rough weather and hard winds...plucky and reckless...full of resource...bound fast by a hundred immutable customs." A few things have changed since then.

East coast fishermen head out to sea with their nets at sunrise, and their day's work is done by late morning. In these villages in Pahang, there is little for the fishermen to do after lunch but mend their nets or play draughts. The favourite place to while away the afternoon is the cool open verandah. The simple kampong house on stilts, constructed of wood and attap, is well-ventilated by the sea breezes.

Richard Kalvar

Malaysia's beaches are spectacular on the east coast of the Peninsula, dotted as they are with fishing villages like Pantai Subak in Kelantan, *above*, which is well-known for their painted fishing boats. During the northeast monsoon season from November to April, the fishing communities attend to repairing their boats and houses rather than brave the stormy seas. During this season, the seas are calm off the west coast which also boasts spectacular stretches of white sand on the island of Langkawi, *right*, which has developed a holiday resort and has its own airport.

The sign board which hangs at this *madrasah*, an institution for religious education, reminds the young Muslim girls living in Malaysia's ethnically diverse west coast, *opposite*, of the five prayer-times to be observed daily, as well as the times of sunrise and sunset, which mark the beginning and breaking of the fast during the month of Ramadan. Until they are ready to learn the finer precepts of Islamic morality and law, they are taught by the *uztaz* or religious teacher. Different cultures in close proximity is part of what makes Malaysia unique. For the Chinese community, prosperity can always be boosted by carrying out the appropriate luck-bringing ceremonies, such as this traditional Southern Chinese lion dance, *top left*, invited to inaugurate new premises in a village in Prai, on the Peninsula across from Penang. In the same village, *bottom left*, advice on government investment schemes is disseminated through a provincial cooperative, which also supports Malay women learning to develop their business abilities.

Abbas

Abbas

The traditional Malay wedding involves great ceremony and protocol, from the time the proposal is made with a gift of betel leaves, to the time the bridegroom goes to the home of his bride.
The entire village, like this one in Prai, is caught up in the grand affair — the men constructing the temporary sheds and providing the musical entertainment, the women preparing the ceremonial items, decorations and food. At the wedding feast, the women sit apart from the men. The bride's delegation gathers in her room, where her bed is bedecked with ceremonial gifts from the groom's family.

Abbas

Kelantan is famous for its *Gasing Uri, top left*, a large hardwood top, shielded with silver or brass and weighing up to 5.5kg. The top is hurled onto the ground with a smooth, artful stroke of the arm. Once launched, the spinning object is delicately transferred with a bat onto a wooden stand to prolong its revolution which can last for hours. *Bottom left:* This east coast state of Peninsular Malaysia is also famous for its ornate kites, which are judged not only for the duration of flight, but also for their beauty and humming sound, produced by an attached bamboo whistle. If the wind is right, an expertly-crafted moon kite can soar the whole night through. *Right:* This Malay dancer is adorned in traditional silver and gold ornaments and wears a *kain songket*, an ornate sarong woven with golden threads. *Overleaf:* The children in the fishing village of Pantai Subak are watching *wayang kulit*, an Indonesian puppet play. A witty puppet master can interpolate current topics into traditional stories.

Steve Vidler

Steve Vidler

In *Main Puteri* (Malay for 'play the princess'), the ritual of healing assumes a form of sacred theatre. Lulled by the strains of the *rebab*, the healer, usually a male shaman, enters a state of trance 'to play the princess' — acting, singing, dancing and generally conversing with unseen forces. After determining the cause of the patient's illness, he expels the spirit or its baleful influences. Some believe the role of Tok Puteri was initiated by a real princess called Puteri Sa'adong and originally performed by women.

The fishing community of Pulau Ketam, near Klang, whose lives and livelihoods are vulnerable to inclement weather, continue the rituals as practised by their seafaring forefathers of scattering offerings to spirits in the sea during the seventh lunar month (called the month of the Hungry Ghosts). Temple helpers bring the boat out to the location determined by the medium. The ceremony is presided over by a Taoist priest who chants the appropriate verses to appease the spirits of those who drowned at sea.

Jean Gaumy

Jean Gaumy

With its old stevedores and shoe-boats, Kuala Selangor retains a quaint ambience that hints of its history as the state's oldest port. It is the original seat of the Selangor Sultanate, established by the Bugis in the 18th century. The Bugis, a seafaring and warrior race from Sulawesi, were successful in resisting Dutch attempts to control the seaport and its tin trade. Although superseded by Port Klang as the regional port, Kuala Selangor, lying off the west coast highway, is still a station for passenger boats and small traders dealing with the agricultural interior. In Penang, a section of Weld Quay contains a community whose heritage is also linked with the sea, *overleaf*. Their first homes were built on six 'clan jetties', each settled by members of a Chinese clan with the same surname. Their forefathers came over a century ago to work as fishermen, stevedores and boatmen and built homes over the water. Their descendants extended the neighbourhood further into the sea, completing their villages with shops and clan temples.

Jean Gaumy

In the mid-19th century, tin in Perak was exclusively mined by Chinese entrepreneurs. Coolies were brought in to work those labour-intensive mines, carved out in dangerous frontier territory defended by gangs and secret societies. At the turn of the century however, European mining ventures with high-capital technology began to take over. Today the major tin-mines are run by national and multinational companies with sophisticated dredging machines. Operating at marginal profits, small Chinese mines scavenge the ground already covered by the dredging operations.

Gueorgui Pinkhassov

The Datuk Keramat smelting factory in Kampar, Perak, has been in operation since its founding in 1898 by Lee Chin Ho, the first Chinese smelter to use reverberatory furnaces. With a board of directors which included some of the most influential tin miners of Perak, the former Eastern Smelting Company began producing the 'Straits Refined Tin' ingot whose trademark 'ESCOY' has become internationally renowned. Now tin concentrates from all over the world are processed at the company's completely modernised smelting operations.

Chinese street opera or *wayang, these pages,* was a major form of evening entertainment for Malaysian Chinese in the early part of the century. It has lost considerable ground to more contemporary forms of entertainment and is now staged mostly during the Hungry Ghost festival in August/September, or on important community occasions. A *wayang* always brings back to the street life of the urban Chinese a sense of excitement during its two- or three-night performance. Accompanying the *wayang* are hawker stalls selling food to the equally itinerant audiences. *Preceding:* During the month of the Hungry Ghosts, children are taught to pray to the Sky God — *Tian Gong* — to ensure their own personal well-being and future prosperity. At the Kuan Yin (Goddess of Mercy) Temple, the oldest and most popular temple in Penang, such festivals and daily rituals are an intrinsic part of the lives of the majority of Chinese families residing in the extensive old quarter of Georgetown.

Taoists priests march ceremoniously through this Chinese village in Perak, *left*, preceded by noisy gongs and cymbals. Religious events remain an integral part of communal village life, in spite of the growing influence of television and urban entertainment. Village events are often feasts as well, some villagers having grown prosperous from supplying the big cities with rural produce, including poultry.

Oil palm was introduced into Malaysia with massive government schemes and incentives, in an effort to reduce the country's dependency on rubber exports. In the 1970s, millions of hectares of rubber plantations were given over to the planting of oil palm. The West Estate plantation on Carey Island, *preceding*, used to grow rubber. Despite swings in commodity prices, oil palm is still a more profitable crop than rubber, *overleaf*, although its hectarage is less. Malaysia is the world's largest palm oil producer today, exporting some six million tonnes, and its two million hectares of oil palm contribute more than 10 percent to the gross national product. Private oil palm estates provide jobs for more than 250,000 workers, *these pages*, while some 60,000 rural families depend on the 600,000 hectares cultivated under government land schemes for their livelihood.

Ian Berry

Ian Berry

Georg Gerster

Like the coconut, the oil palm is a tree of a hundred uses. Nothing is wasted — its oil is used for cooking and confectionery and detergent manufacturing; its trunk for blackboards; its effluent processed into gas for fuel, fertiliser and animal fodder. Until the development of Peninsular Malaysia's North-South highway, *right*, the plantation home such as that in Guthrie's Tanah Merah Oil Palm Estate in Sepang, Perak, *above*, had few modern amenities. Nevertheless, the estate manager was able to enjoy a high standard of living.

Karl Ammann

The Negritos, *these pages*, the only truly nomadic tribe of Orang Asli, live in the Cameron Highlands of Pahang, *preceding*. They practise no cultivation and have few possessions since mobility has priority. Their forefathers were hunters and gatherers who lived in caves and rock shelters. Cameron Highlands is one of Malaysia's many hill stations where tea plantations and vegetable gardens flourish. As a temperate highland resort, it was opened only after 1885, when government surveyor William Cameron found "a fine plateau with gentle slopes shut in by the mountains".

Jean Gaumy

On Carey Island, in the delta of the Selangor River, an Orang Asli group called the Mah Meri share the island with a large palm oil plantation. The Mah Meri number little over one thousand today. An Orang Asli museum in Gombak preserves their records and artefacts and these Mah Meri girls, *above and right*, wearing masks and dresses made of tree bark and coconut fronds, perform their magical dances for tourists.

Dennis Lau

The Malay term *ulu* (meaning the upper reaches of a river) refers to far more than geography. To many coastal people it describes a way of life that gets more primitive, alien and unattractive the farther inland one goes. The Penan of Sarawak are a group that suffer from the *ulu* concept. They are nomads of the rainforest whom distant bureaucrats want to 'civilise' so that they can enjoy the benefits that other Malaysians enjoy. *Opposite:* Laka Ama (with beard) from Long (meaning confluence, as 'kuala' in Malay) Melamun and Wan Mun (with hat) from Long Balau visit the son of Penan headman Agan Polisi. *Left:* the headman's daughter and grandson share some bread with a pet monkey.

Dennis Lau

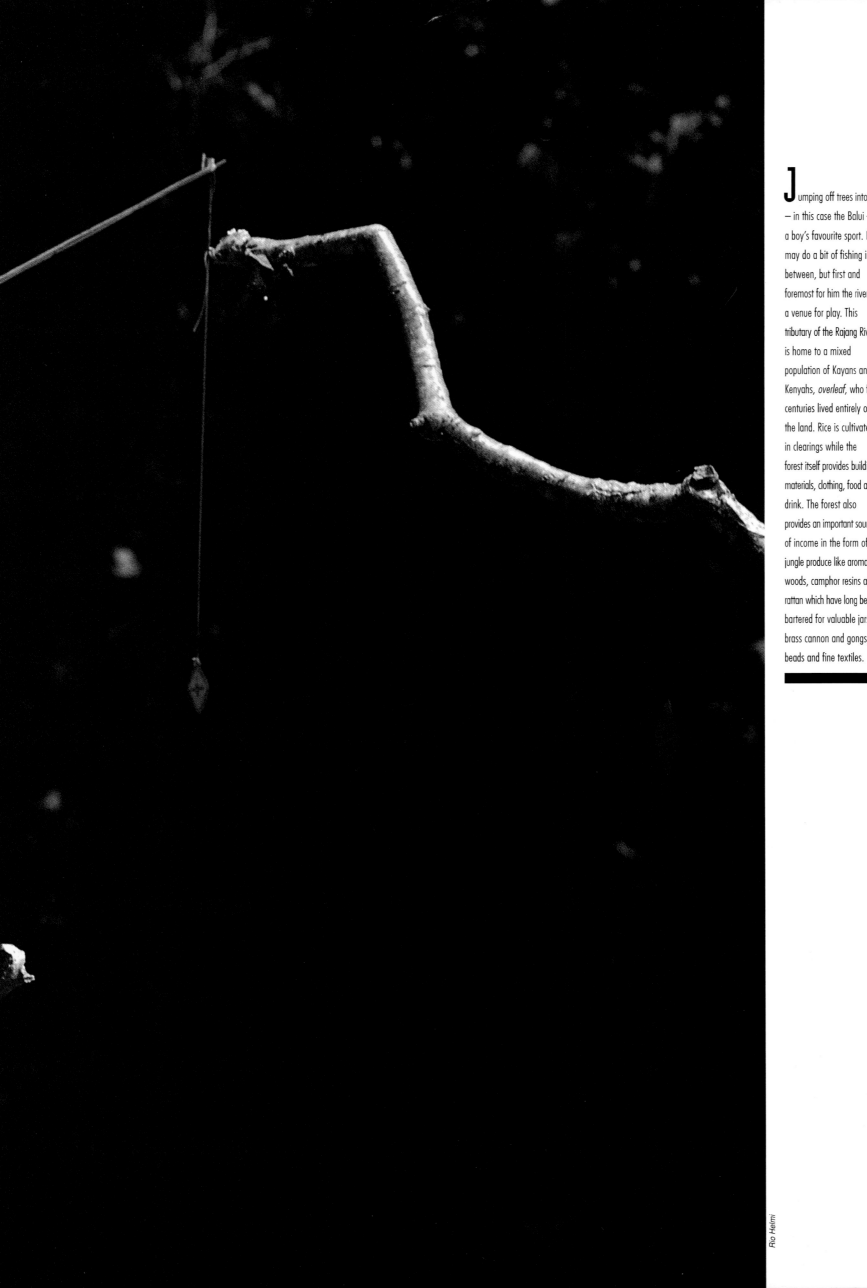

Jumping off trees into a river — in this case the Balui — is a boy's favourite sport. He may do a bit of fishing in between, but first and foremost for him the river is a venue for play. This tributary of the Rajang River is home to a mixed population of Kayans and Kenyahs, *overleaf*, who for centuries lived entirely off the land. Rice is cultivated in clearings while the forest itself provides building materials, clothing, food and drink. The forest also provides an important source of income in the form of jungle produce like aromatic woods, camphor resins and rattan which have long been bartered for valuable jars, brass cannon and gongs, beads and fine textiles.

Safely nestled in his back cradle, this young Kayan, *right*, looks at the world with slightly critical eyes. Mother is contentedly smoking a home-made cigar while father risks life and limb daily earning a livelihood for them as a logger.

Leonard Lueras

These longhouse children in Ulu Ai have an easy life, as Ibans indulge their children fully. Boys do what they like, and nothing they dislike, and grown-ups will interrupt their work if a child clamours for attention. While village boys play in the river or explore the surrounding forests, their sisters look after the younger siblings while their parents work in the rice fields. However, school cuts into this freedom, bringing with it new ideas and aspirations into the traditional Bornean life.

Iban women are the best weavers in Borneo and skilled weavers hold a high place in the longhouse, being the female counterpart of warriors. Just as a young man had to take an enemy head to prove himself before marriage, a girl was considered eligible for marriage only after she had woven one *pua kumbu*, a length of textile fashioned with artistry and displayed in family rooms during festivals. Offerings are presented on it, including, in the old days, head trophies.

No Iban ceremony is complete without a *miring*, an offering of food for the gods spread on a new mat or *pua kumbu*. If the rite is important, an elder is invited to bless the gifts and the assembled company with a fowl, *right*; for informal occasions, a young man may be trusted with the task. The most important event in Iban religious life is the *gawai*, a festival where the gods are invited to attend a lavish feast held in their honour. Naughty longhouse children may be frightened into obedience with an ugly mask worn by a friend of the family, *above*.

About a quarter of East Malaysia's 3.3 million population are Christians. The first Anglican Mission in Sarawak was set up in 1848. Today, the Anglican, Roman Catholic, Methodist and Evangelical churches are staffed by local priests and pastors. *Right:* Traditions die hard in Sarawak, and this Kelabit from Bareo, a devout Christian, finds nothing wrong with wearing the tooth of the fiercest animal in the Borneo rainforest, the clouded leopard, as a sign of his masculinity. Girls with long earlobes can have a little operation, snipping them back to normal length when they go to school.

Unlike the dwellings of most other Bornean peoples, Kelabit longhouses do not have separate family apartments divided from one another by party walls. Instead, they have an open plan design, but each family has a clearly defined space demarcated by floor mats around the hearths running along the centre spine of the longhouse. The Kelabits are a society in transition. Many of the bright young people have gone 'downriver'. Academic success carries its own reward — a coveted government job. Some take their aged parents to live with them in town, while others visit the longhouse during festivals, bringing gifts and contributions to the parental household.

Mike Yamashita

No celebration in Kemabong would be complete without the heady rice brew called *tapai*. Made of glutinous rice and yeast, the drink is common to indigenous Borneo people. While other Sabahans drink *tapai* from a glass or bamboo container, the Muruts, *far left*, have discovered the shortcut of using a substantial straw. The faster he finishes the *tapai* in the antique stoneware jar, the better. These Tagals, *left*, a sub-group of the Muruts, enjoy a traditional game of leaping on springy platforms to get a prize from the rafters.

The Rungus, *these pages*, live in the northern parts of Sabah, on Kudat Peninsula and 'between the ears' for those who see Borneo as a fat dragon on the map of Southeast Asia. They are a sub-group of Sabah's predominant Kadazan-Dusun peoples who cling to their traditional way of life with some tenacity. Many Rungus live in longhouses like Mompilis, and retain their animistic beliefs.

From the sea this Bajau Laut village of Kampong Serusuk in Sabah looks as if it was surrounded by water. There are gangplanks from the back kitchens to the shore — escape routes in case of fire or, in the old days, attack from the sea. Life on the stilts is like life in any kampong. The daily portion of rice is polished in a hardwood mortar, only here the husk is not pecked up by pigs and chickens under the house. These children, *left*, inherit a way of living on the water that is hundreds of years old. Their parents paddle to the shore to tend farms and bury the dead, but they look to the sea for protection and their daily diet of fish.

Nomachi

177

Sempoma lies on the east coast of Sabah, one of the few places in Malaysia where small craft at sea are in some danger of pirate attack. An amphibious population lives in huts built in the shallows, on the big fishtraps, and on houseboats. Fish is the common food here; the area's salt fish is famous throughout the region.

Tommy Chang

Tommy Chang

In the 19th century, sago was one of Sarawak's principal export crops. The Melanau farmers of Kampong Tilian fell their tall sago palms when the trunks swell, prior to flowering. They are kept in rafts on the river to soften, *right*. The starch-bearing pith is rasped, *top left*, leached and left to settle in sedimentation troughs. It is sun-dried on large mats to produce raw sago flour. As a staple, sago is cooked to soft porridge consistency. Crunchy pellets are baked on a wood-fired clay hearth in the villages, *bottom left*, or by sophisticated machinery in factories.

Mengkabong is one of many villages on the water which fringe the Sabah coast. Some of these picturesque shanty-towns house indigenous Bajaus, others a semi-mobile regional population of illegal immigrants that is beginning to settle in Sabah. The number of illegal immigrants is estimated at 200,000 to 500,000. Malaysian administrators point out that they make unscheduled demands on the State's medical, educational and health services.

Ara Güler

The wall of a chettiar restaurant in Malacca, *right*, reveals the characteristic preoccupations of the older members of Malaysia's Indian community — a portrait of national unity hangs alongside images of an Indian film star politician, a Hindu goddess and Mahatma Gandhi. The most common meal is still that of rice, curry and dhal; prepared in aluminum pots, served on banana leaf, and eaten with the right hand. *Above:* Malaysian children benefit from a wide range of social services. The government encourages a high birth-rate in order to achieve its target population of 70 million.

Some of the region's specialties can only be sampled at rickety little tables under canvas or leaf awnings. The ubiquitous food hawkers of Malaysia are what makes eating out such an adventure because of the variety of meals available. Meat skewered on stems of coconut leaves sizzles over charcoal grills. Chicken wings await a final browning. Noodles and dumplings and patties and cakes are offered as snacks at roadside tables. During the fasting month of Ramadan, a night market springs up in every Malay village.

Paul Chesley

Paul Chesley

The Straits Chinese or Peranakans have made a significant contribution to Malaysian cuisine and culture. Their women or *nonyas*, many of whom still wear *sarong* and *kebaya*, *above*, are traditionally good cooks, and their delectable cuisine is a fusion of Malay, Chinese and Indian flavours. *Nonya* cooking, *left*, no longer relies on manual preparation of spices and ingredients — an elaborate process made possible in the old days by a large retinue of kitchen help.

Nicholas Devore

Michelangelo Durazzo

Gerald Gay

Dominic Sansoni

Luca I. Tettoni

Luca I. Tettoni

Gerald Gay

Food in Malaysia is not only tasty in all its multi-racial range but also colourful, whether for human or — as in the case of the *top left* picture — spiritual consumption. Sometimes, dishes such as chilli crab, *centre left*, and *kueh* or cakes, *bottom left*, are a blend of *Nonya* and Malay styles of cooking. Chinese snacks like *char siew pow*, *centre*, are now made both by individual vendors as well as manufactured by food factories, as are the salt eggs, *top centre*, which the Chinese eat with congee. In villages and smaller towns, colourful soft drinks are still sold by push-cart vendor, *top right*.

Basil Pao

Among the traders who flocked to Penang in the 18th century were the Straits Chinese from Malacca who were lured to the duty-free port founded by Francis Light. Today, Penang, along with the former Straits Settlements of Malacca and Singapore, remains one of the three centres of *Peranakan* culture, which is alive and thriving as the *nonya — above —* shows in her traditional attire. Her forefathers moved from Malacca after that port declined under restrictive Dutch trade policies. The Dutch built their own church in Malacca, *left*, ensuring a memorial to their 150-year occupation.

193

A significant proportion of Malaysia's 1.6 million Indians are Hindus and their temples dot both the rural and urban areas. This Indian woman is praying in the Sri Mahamariamman temple in Batu Caves just outside Kuala Lumpur. Hindus observe a variety of festivals, the most important being Deepavali and Thaipusam. Hundreds of thousands of Hindu devotees flock to the Sri Mahamariamman temple at Thaipusam to commemorate the birth of the Lord Subramaniam. The festival is celebrated with the fervour of the Mardi Gras. The temple has a cave shrine 272 steps up, where offerings of thanksgiving and penance are made.

Ian Berry

A Hindu wedding is elaborate in costume, rites and detail. Usually solemnised in a temple with a priest in attendance, chanting Sanskrit prayers and making offerings of camphor, ghee, pulses, fruits and flowers. The bridegroom fastens the *tali* — the matrimonial chain — around his bride's neck. Hindu wedding rites include the exchange of garlands, clothes, jewellery and money; or, as is still practised, the giving of dowry; and the placing of toe rings on the bride.

Ian Berry

Ian Berry

The century-old Vivekanda Ashram in Brickfields, Kuala Lumpur, provides education for underprivileged children of Indian descent, including those from rural areas. It is also a centre for socio-religious and cultural activities, including the Sutra dance group. This group exemplifies the multi-cultural blend that makes Malaysia's art scene exciting. Group leader Ramli Ibrahim, a Malay, has mastered the rigorous discipline of Indian dance and draws dancers from each of Malaysia's main ethnic groups.

Raghu Rai

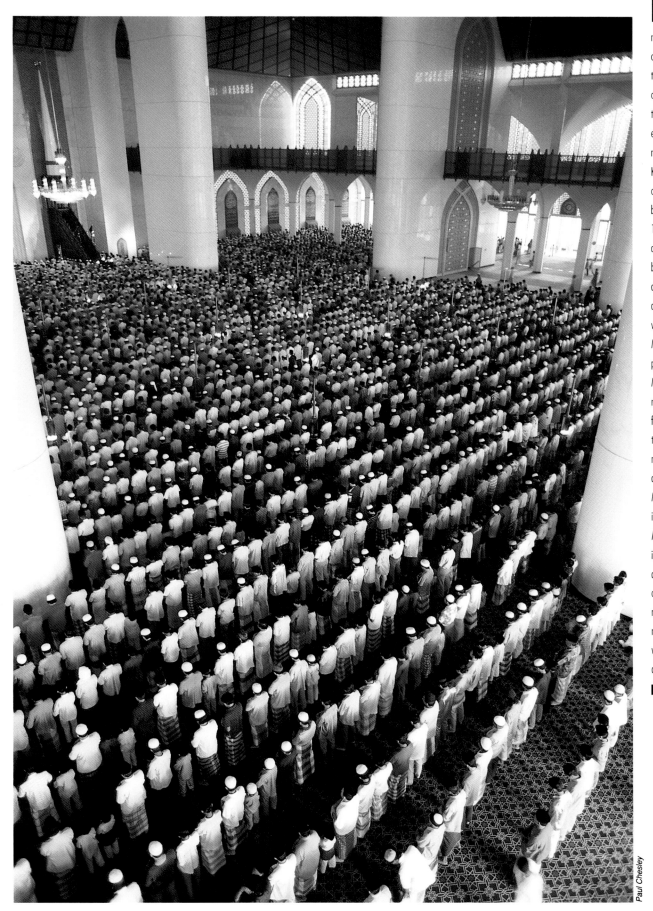

Islam is Malaysia's state religion, with 51 per cent of the 17 million people — the Malays — Muslims. The construction of mosques in the country follows economic prosperity. The new state mosque in Kuching, *opposite*, which cost US$15.5 million to build, was completed in 1990. Its attractive architectural style is said to be symbolic, the blue main dome signifying heaven and the 40 smaller domes within it the age when Mohammed became a prophet. While Islam in Malaysia bears little relation to the fundamentalism of sects in the Middle East, the religion does set the Malay apart from his fellow Malaysians: Friday, for instance is a day of prayer, *left*, and alcohol and pork is forbidden. Laxity in attending Friday prayers or other backsliding does not mean any erosion of religious belief. Foreigners who marry Malays must accept the faith of Islam.

Paul Chesley

The State Mosque in Kota Kinabalu, capital of Sabah, boasts fine modern Islamic architecture, combining traditional and modern lines. One of Kota Kinabalu's few architectural attractions, it has a large honeycomb dome supported by massive pillars topped with smaller golden domes. Built in 1976, the mosque houses offices and a meeting hall for 1,200 people on the ground floor; the first floor accommodates 5,000 male devotees while the second floor has room for 500 female devotees.

Ian Berry

Standing in the commercial centre of Kuala Lumpur is the 38-storey headquarters of the Pilgrim Fund Management Board, whose architecture combines religious and secular considerations. Among the Five Pillars of Islam which form the religious base for every Muslim is the duty to make the pilgrimage to Mecca, the *haj*. Muslim men who have made the pilgrimage are accorded the honorific *Haji* and women *Hajjah*. The Board helps with the organisation and expense of the *haj*.

Paul Chesley

Muslim religious schools like the Tadika Ehsan in Shah Alam, *above,* in Selangor promote religious education starting with the very young. At these schools, the children are taught to recite the Koran even if the Arabic text is only imperfectly understood. Also in Shah Alam is the largest mosque in Southeast Asia, the Sultan Salahuddin Abdul Aziz Mosque, named after the incumbent Sultan of Selangor, the interior of which is pictured *left.*

205

Dominic Sansoni

The majority of Chinese in Malaysia are bound to a tradition of ancestor worship, Confucian ethics and Taoist supernaturalism but they turn to the Buddhas and the Bodhisatvas for spiritual consolation and mental peace. Most Chinese Buddhists adhere to the Mahayana School. At the Cheng Hoon Teng or Temple of Pure Clouds in Malacca, *these pages*, priests comfortably supported by temple devotees dedicate their lives to the acquisition of merit through chanting and meditation, and practise calligraphy during breaks.

207

To strengthen diplomatic ties between China and the Malacca Sultanate in the 16th century, a notable Ming-dynasty admiral brought a 500-strong delegation to settle in Malacca. The first generation intermarried with the locals, assimilating with the Malay culture and language. The original community spread to Penang and Singapore when the former British Straits Settlements were founded. Many of the Straits Chinese today can trace their ancestry in this country to over a dozen generations. Of the many fine and ornate Chinese temples they constructed, the oldest is Malacca's Cheng Hoon Teng or Temple of Pure Clouds, which dates back to 1646.

Patrick Zachmann

The Chinese festival of the Hungry Ghosts begins on the 1st and lasts until the 30th of the seventh lunar month. During this period, families visit and clean their ancestor's graves on odd calendar days. They burn offerings of food, paper money and reproductions of clothing, cars and furniture to their departed relatives and spirits in general. Incense is burned and candles lit to guide the ghosts to the banquet which they are supposed to enjoy. During ceremonial offerings, mediums work themselves into a trance to communicate with spirits.

211

Once Kuala Lumpur's largest 'wet' market, Central Market has become the capital's most successful tourist effort, *opposite*. A major focal point for local culture including fortune-telling, *bottom left*, arts and crafts, it features performances by musicians, dancers and foreign troupes, as well as dog shows, *top left*. The 50-year-old art deco building, with its old facade and a massive skylight is a prime example of architectural preservation. In the heart of the city, its bazaar atmosphere has made it a crowd puller.

Steve Vidler

Steve McCurry

217

RSATUAN TUKANG JAHIT WILAYAH PERSEKUTUAN SELANGOR

雪 隆 縫 業 公 會

THE SELANGOR FEDERAL TERRITORY TAILORS GUILD

SDN. BHD

Paul Chesley

In Kuala Lumpur's Chinatown, *above*, a wide range of trades spills over the sidewalks and one can find pet shops — birds are popular — next to funeral parlours. *Right:* Islamic tradition requires Muslim women to show modesty in their attire and in Malaysia many cover their heads and wear the *baju kurong*, a traditional Malay dress form. Conservative attire, however, does not mean young Malay women who work — like this petrol station attendant — cannot make practical adaptations to their work clothes.

Bruno Barbey

Downtown Kuala Lumpur, the administrative and business capital of Malaysia, is a collage of 20th-century skyscrapers and 19th-century Moghul architecture. The city's oldest mosque, Masjid Jame, *left*, stands at the confluence of the Gombak and Batu Rivers. Its design by AB Hubback was adapted from a Moghul mosque in northern India. *Above:* The Sultan Abdul Samad building is Kuala Lumpur's most photographed landmark. Once the headquarters of the colonial secretariat, it now houses the Supreme Court. It flanks Merdeka Square, the historical heart of the city.

221

The Proton Saga, launched by the government in 1985 as the first all-Malaysian car, is being intensively marketed both locally and internationally. The country's pilot car manufacturing project was undertaken as a joint venture between a national corporation HICOM and Japan's Mitsubishi group. The greater objective was to introduce high-technology to the country's heavy industry, with the intention of generating related industrial projects in the near future. At the car plant in Shah Alam, Japanese car-making technology will be entirely run by Malaysians.

Paul Chesley

225

Malaysian uniformed forces include the police, *left*, and an all-volunteer armed forces, of which the 13,000-strong navy forms a part, *right*. Together with the army and air force, the navy has undergone rapid expansion and modernisation to achieve the objective of self-reliance in defence of the nation. On National Day — August 31 — they take their salute at Merdeka (independence) Square.

Steve McCurry

Malaysia is a constitutional monarchy, and the rulers of nine out of the country's thirteen states are sovereign monarchs or Sultans. The King or Yang di-Pertuan Agong, is elected by his brother rulers once in five years. In 1990, the King was Sultan Azlan Shah of Perak; accompanied at official functions by the Queen or the Raja Permaisuri Agong. Known as the most highly qualified ruler in the country's history, Sultan Azlan Shah previously held the position of Lord President of the Malaysian judiciary.

Overleaf: The Malaysian flag symbolises the spirit of solidarity (in the canton of dark blue) and peace — the 14 red and white stripes stand for the equal status of the Federal Government and the 13 member states of Johor, Kedah, Kelantan, Malacca, Negri Sembilan, Pahang, Penang, Perak, Perlis, Sabah, Sarawak, Selangor and Trengganu. The crescent is the symbol of Islam, the state religion, and the star points to the unity of the states within the Federal Government. Yellow is the royal colour of the Malay rulers.

Rene Burri

229

4

ANNEXES

Many people had proposed a big photographic book on Malaysia, a beautiful land that so many see in so many different ways. But it is hard to pinpoint exactly when the idea of this particular project became reality. Was it when Didier Millet, publisher of *Indonesia: A Voyage through the Archipelago* and *Thailand: Seven Days in the Kingdom*, invited Austen Zecha of AMC-Melewar Zecha Communications to Bali in September 1989? Or when Zecha and Marina Mahathir-Roussille met Yvan Van Outrive and Luca Tettoni in Bangkok three months after that? Or when seven prominent Malaysians were invited to be members of an Editorial Advisory Board? Or was it when the first press conference to announce the project was held on a stormy afternoon in March 1990, after which there was really no going back? When the "shoot" should take place was decided fairly early on — it would be the week of August 28 to September 3, 1990 which would cover Malaysia's National Day, August 31, planned to be extra-grand for 1990's Visit Malaysia Year.

The first priority was to look for sponsors — necessary for a project as massive and expensive as this. Project Director Mahathir-Roussille had the task of gathering corporate sponsors. The first to be approached was YTL Corporation, who quickly saw the potential of such a project and how much a book like this was needed in Malaysia. They readily agreed. Other sponsors reacted similarly. Not all the sponsors gave cash. Malaysia Airlines provided the huge number of tickets needed to fly photographers and staff to, from and around Malaysia. Kodak was a natural ally. Alberto del Hoyo, General Manager of The Regent of Kuala Lumpur, was quick to appreciate the appeal of a book like this one.

The other sponsors fell into place almost as easily. The shoot was to begin in Kuala Lumpur and end in Kuching, Sarawak so that the photographers could get a taste of both Peninsular and East Malaysia, two very different parts of the country. The Ministry of Tourism and Environment, Sarawak, eagerly agreed to host the whole group in Kuching. The Kuching Hilton's General Manager, Wolfgang Maier, had been involved in Millet's Indonesia book the previous year and was happy to repeat the experience.

Meanwhile, in the Paris office of Editions Didier Millet, faxes were sent all over the world inviting photographers to join in the project. With so many renowned photographers interested, it was very difficult to narrow the choice down to the 46 finally selected to capture a week of Malaysian life on film.

Luca Tettoni, Chief Photographer, and Peter Schoppert, Project Editor, made scouting trips to map out the various assignments for the photographers. Editorial Advisory Board members were informed of developments and provided extremely useful ideas, leads and contacts.

In Mahathir-Roussille's office, Irene Tan, Transport Coordinator, had started to work out the flight logistics with Belinda Davies, the Project Coordinator in Paris. Mahathir-Roussille began to look for enthusiastic and energetic people to become assignment coordinators who would work out the logistics of each photographer's assignment. June Yunos, a tiny bundle of energy with experience in staging shows at Club Med was put in charge of all the photographers assigned to the Peninsula's East Coast. Chris Lee and June Baharuddin, freelancers from the advertising world, took Kuala Lumpur and event coordination respectively.

In June, Davies arrived in Kuala Lumpur and took charge of the awesome task of coordinating all the photographers' transport and accommodation requirements. The assignment coordinators — including Khoo Su Nin who was responsible for the West Coast of Peninsular Malaysia and Jim Holloway for Sabah and Sarawak — filled up the office with their maps, books and guides. Telephone calls and faxes went all over Malaysia requesting information and seeking permission to photograph odd nooks and crannies.

Mahathir-Roussille and Baharuddin worked on planning the many events to take place once the photographers arrived. Karen Roberts, director of promotions at AMC, lent a hand in organising several newsworthy events and photo opportunities. Two press conferences were held to announce the sponsors of the project. The first showed the six Diamond Sponsors presenting their cheques. The second was for the 14 Gold Sponsors. People began to notice that a major event was in the offing . . .

Two weeks before the photographers arrived, the project team moved into their headquarters at The Regent, a large luxurious room where desks, Apple Macs, white boards, charts and of course, the vital coffee machine, were set up. This nerve centre of the Project was quickly nicknamed the 'nervous centre' because of the nerves that were stretched taut – but never snapped.

Janie Joseland Bennett arrived from Aspen, Colorado, to help with the vital computer programming of the various schedules. Caroline Goh, Events Coordinator for East Malaysia, called in almost daily to report on the Sarawak programme. The last two sponsors signed up.

Then the photographers began to arrive. Each was briefed on the assignment and given a bag of films and Malaysian souvenirs. Last-minute adjustments were made to individual itineraries. Friendships were renewed or made. The Project HQ became like a clubhouse, with photographers, project team members and visitors wandering in and out, chatting, drinking endless cups of coffee and glasses of wine.

On Friday, August 24, a 'steamboat' dinner was held at the Royal Selangor Club in the centre of Kuala Lumpur for photographers and team members. Amidst a lot of laughter, a very embarrassed Mahathir-Roussille was presented with a plaque declaring her "Marina: Sweetheart of Southeast Asia".

The next morning's press conference introducing the photographers ended with a ceremony conducted by members of the Mah Meri Orang Asli community from Carey Island, Selangor, conferring traditional blessings. Immediately after the press conference, a convoy of twenty Proton Sagas (Malaysia's national car) escorted by out-riders made its way through the streets of Kuala Lumpur towards Sri Perdana, official residence of the Prime Minister of Malaysia. They were hosted to a typical Malaysian lunch by the Prime Minister, Dato Seri Dr Mahathir Mohamad and his wife, Datin Seri Dr Siti Hasmah, where a variety of food was cooked fresh at hawker stalls. The photographers found the Prime Minister relaxed and congenial, asking them many questions about photography and not only allowing himself to be photographed but also taking photographs of his guests.

In the evening, Kodak held a welcoming cocktail. On Sunday morning everyone was herded by Luca Tettoni to Kuala Lumpur's Lake Gardens for the traditional group photograph. The Regent of Kuala Lumpur hosted a gala dinner for the photographers on Sunday night – an enormous buffet set at the poolside. Four dance groups displayed the best of Malaysian culture.

At 4:30 am the next day, the first group left the hotel. As dawn broke, others began to make their way towards their destinations throughout the country, via car or airplane. For the photographers, an early start was crucial: after an hour of sunshine, tropical light becomes harsh and contrasty.

In the Project HQ, the team started preparing for the end of the shoot, the photographers' debriefing and their departure from Malaysia. Staff members also had to be on standby in case photographers called in with problems. On the first day of the shoot there were plenty of these. On Friday, August 31, National Day, the team shifted operation – complete with an impressive cargo of files and computers and other project paraphernalia – to Kuching.

On Sunday, September 2, after two more spectacular parties on the Kuching River, assignment coordinators sat down to retrieve film from tired and bedraggled photographers, collect their roll notes and debrief each one, all this under the cine lights of a crew shooting a video about the making of the book. Three different camera-teams had in fact been following the photographers on their assignments for the same purpose.

At the press conference the next morning, the photographers concurred that, on the whole, it had been a successful week's photography, in spite of the less than ideal weather which plagued the project even on the last night, forcing the cancellation of a cruise up the Sarawak River but not a good party at the Sarawak Cultural Village.

Back at the hotel, staff and photographers lingered in the lobby, reluctant to say goodbye too soon. Addresses and phone numbers were exchanged and farewells were sad and heartfelt. "This was really the best-organised project," said one photographer. "It feels like one big happy family," declared another. Many promised to return. They had seen things in a memorable week that they wanted to explore further, knowing that in Malaysia lay an undiscovered gem of adventure.

Cartoons by LAT of Gavin Young, *opposite top*; project team, *opposite bottom*; Paul Wachtel, *bottom right*.
Top right: Prime Minister Dato Seri Dr Mahathir Mohamad and Marina Mahathir-Roussille.

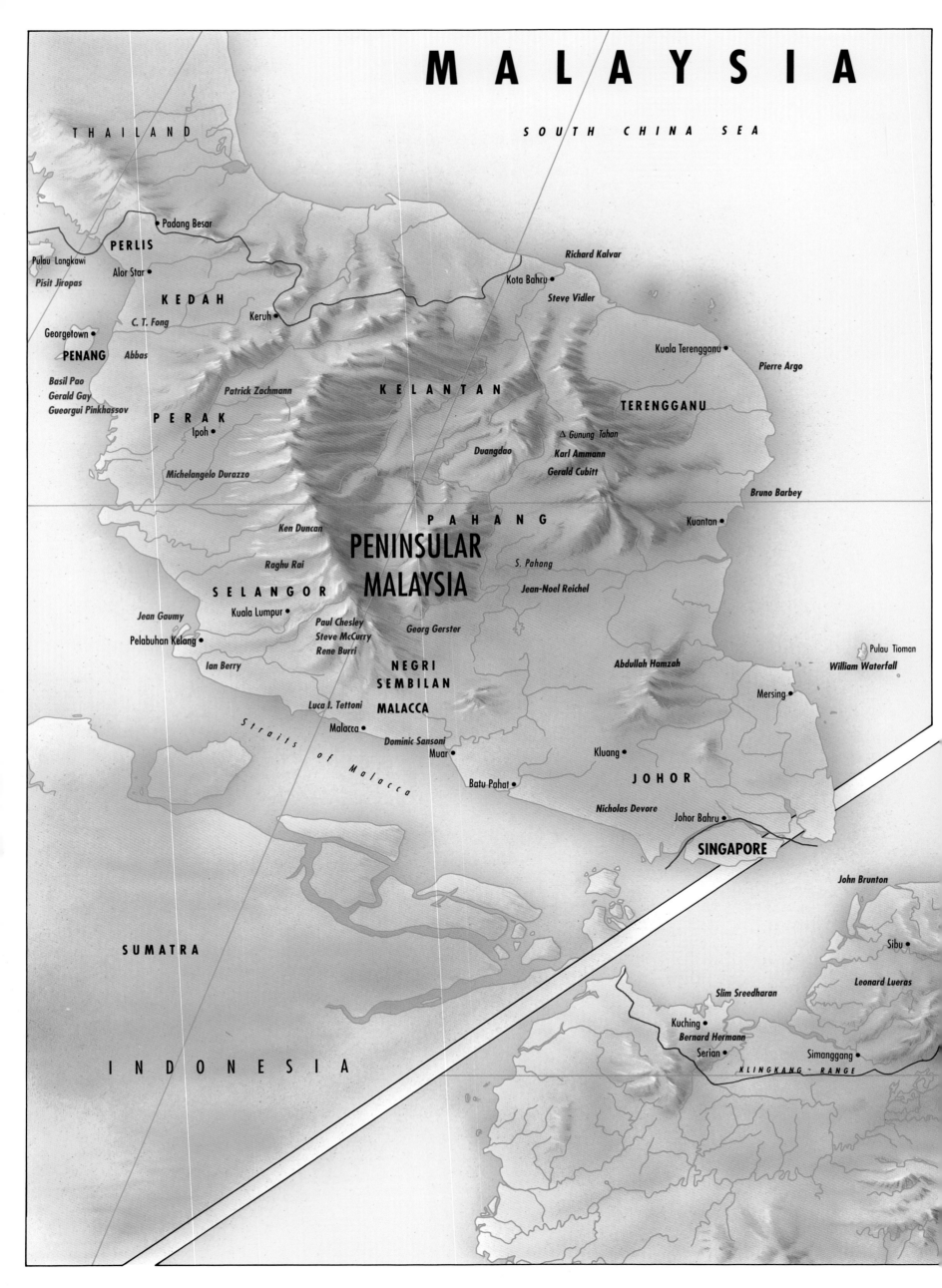

MALAYSIA

SOUTH CHINA SEA

THAILAND

Padang Besar •

PERLIS

Pulau Langkawi

Pisit Jiropas

Alor Star •

KEDAH

C. T. Fong

Keruh •

Richard Kalvar

Kota Bahru •

Steve Vidler

Georgetown •

Abbas

PENANG

Basil Pao
Gerald Gay
Gueorgui Pinkhassov

Patrick Zachmann

KELANTAN

Kuala Terengganu •

Pierre Argo

PERAK

Ipoh •

TERENGGANU

△ Gunung Tahan

Karl Ammann

Michelangelo Durazzo

Duangdao

Gerald Cubitt

Bruno Barbey

Ken Duncan

PAHANG

Kuantan •

PENINSULAR
MALAYSIA

Raghu Rai

S. Pahang

SELANGOR

Jean-Noel Reichel

Jean Gaumy

Kuala Lumpur •

Paul Chesley
Steve McCurry
Rene Burri

Georg Gerster

Pelabuhan Kelang •

Pulau Tioman

Abdullah Hamzah

William Waterfall

Ian Berry

**NEGRI
SEMBILAN**

Mersing •

Luca I. Tettoni

MALACCA

Malacca •

Dominic Sansoni

Muar •

Kluang •

JOHOR

Batu Pahat •

Nicholas Devore

Johor Bahru •

Straits of Malacca

SINGAPORE

John Brunton

SUMATRA

Sibu •

Slim Sreedharan

Leonard Lueras

Kuching •

Bernard Hermann

Serian •

Simanggang •

INDONESIA

KLINGKANG RANGE

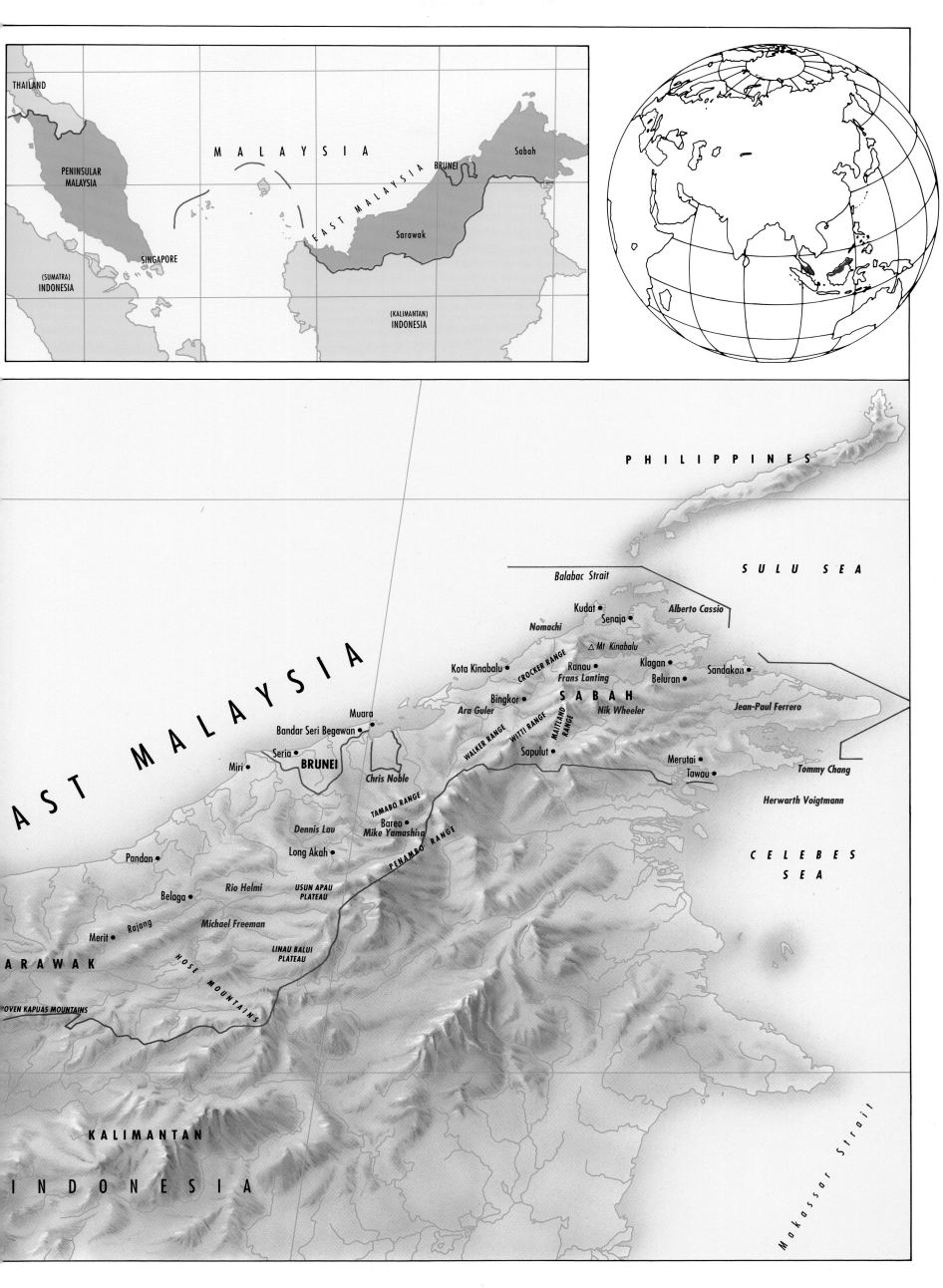

THAILAND

MALAYSIA

PENINSULAR
MALAYSIA

SINGAPORE

(SUMATRA)
INDONESIA

EAST MALAYSIA

BRUNEI

Sabah

Sarawak

(KALIMANTAN)
INDONESIA

PHILIPPINES

SULU SEA

Balabac Strait

Kudat
Senaja
Nomachi
Alberto Cassio

△ Mt Kinabalu

Kota Kinabalu
CROCKER RANGE
Ranau
Frans Lanting
Klagan
Beluran
Sandakan

Bingkor
SABAH
Nik Wheeler
Jean-Paul Ferrero

Ara Guler
WALKER RANGE
WITTI RANGE
MAITLAND RANGE
Sapulut
Merutai
Tawau
Tommy Chang

Muara
Bandar Seri Begawan

Seria
BRUNEI

Miri

Chris Noble

Herwarth Voigtmann

TAMABO RANGE
PENAMBO RANGE

Bareo
Mike Yamashina

CELEBES
SEA

Dennis Lau

Long Akah

Pandan

Belaga
Rio Helmi
USUN APAU
PLATEAU

Michael Freeman

Merit
Rajang
LINAU BALUI
PLATEAU

HOSE MOUNTAINS

RAWAK

OVEN KAPUAS MOUNTAINS

KALIMANTAN

INDONESIA

Makassar Strait

EAST MALAYSIA

The last day of August. Late in the morning, Gerald Gay is scouring the market stalls of Penang's Chinatown for the perfect jackfruit. Perfect, that is, in appearance, for this will complete the list of props that he needs to orchestrate a still-life food shot. The cooking has already started at the house of a local Straits Chinese family, but it will take Gay another three hours of work to position the studio lights, refine the arrangement of dishes and check the minutest details of everything on the table.

At the same time, Ken Duncan is driving past ranks of rubber trees in a plantation close to Ipoh, debating with himself whether the glimpse he caught a kilometre back of an old Indian woman tapping a tree is worth shooting. The light tips the balance for him. The haze that has been drifting over the peninsula all week filters the sun through the trees; what could easily have been a harsh contrast of shadow and sunlight has become subtle and atmospheric. He brakes, turns the car round, and returns to set up his panoramic camera.

Exactly one thousand miles to the east, Chris Noble and his assistant Jim Zellers have left the last trace of daylight a mile and a half behind. Working their way slowly up a channel in the heart of Mount Mulu, using the fluted limestone ridges as handholds, they are approaching the Sarawak Chamber, the world's largest underground cavern. Their only illumination is from their helmet lamps, and in the completely saturated atmosphere, the beams penetrate only some 15m through hanging water vapour. In the heat, humidity and running water, they are completely sodden, and it is a major effort to keep the camera equipment dry. They have already this morning had to complete a difficult traverse along the edge of a pool 12 to 15m in diameter, first swimming across to fix a rope along one wall, then

returning to use this as a support while balancing the backpacks on their chests.

Turning their heads from side to side so that the lamp beams swing across the darkness ahead is the only way to keep some idea of where they are in the network of walls, talus slopes and channels. As Noble's beam sweeps across a rock face, it picks out red-gold points of light. This is the eye-flash from the retinas of giant predatory Huntsman spiders, bodies the size of a golfball and a leg span of more than nine inches — and poisonous. The channel narrows, and Zellers puts his left hand out to brace himself against the wall. By reflex he turns his head to check the hold, and recoils suddenly, his hand inches away from one of the spiders. A disabling bite is the last thing that the caving team needs here.

Gay, Duncan and Noble were three among 46 photographers recruited from 18 countries to make a unique piece of reportage — a simultaneous visual record of Malaysia in one week in 1990. Months of preparation had involved a planning team of seven choosing a spread of places, events and people that together would give a special view of this sprawling, varied country. Malaysia's position — maritime yet on the edge of the continent — has made it a land of surprises and contrasts, both in the environment and in human settlement, and this was a matter of particular concern in planning the photography. The country has had an exotic appeal for photographers every bit as much as for writers like Conrad and Maugham, but the degree of

Top: Ken Duncan, *bottom:* Gerald Gay

these contrasts has resisted a single, comprehensive view in pictures. The range, from the shy fauna of the deep rainforest to the kaleidoscope of ethnic communities in the towns, has always been too great for one person to embrace.

The solution for this project lay in choosing the aspects of Malaysia which, taken together would convey a sense of the country's diversity, and then finding the photographers best suited to exploring them. There were three obvious themes — the nature, peoples and traditions — and in the research that began early in the year the editors looked for locations and assignments that would include both the typical and the idiosyncratic. Then, rather than simply turn loose a crowd of cameramen in all directions to see what would happen, the photographers for Malaysia were selected with an eye for their particular abilities. The assignments were matched as closely as possible to the speciality of each, and among 46 photographers there were 46 different skills and styles.

Malaysia's natural environment is arguably its greatest treasure — one that is, like elsewhere, under great pressure. The controversy that surrounds the future of Malaysia's unique rainforests only heightened the importance of doing it justice, and some of the world's most renowned nature photographers were recruited, including specialists in rainforest, aerial photography, diving and caving. The difficulties they experienced in capturing images of once-abundant animals added a poignancy to the project.

The complex history of settlement on the peninsula and Borneo has produced an ethnic and cultural mixture no less varied than the flora and fauna. One of photography's most important documentary roles has been the portrayal of human life in all its aspects. Here in Malaysia, the diverse range of peoples made it especially important to use photographers who were familiar either with the region or with the traditions of particular types of community. More than this, there was a need to show aspects of culture that are now becoming rare

and increasingly confined to special occasions. Certain events had to be organised, and handled by photographers who were used to conceptualising and directing — yet one more type of skill that the editors had to call on.

For the Malaysian photographers Tommy Chang, CT Fong, Abdullah Hamzah and Dennis Lau this was home ground; for many of the others it was a new and sometimes strange experience. Photography in the tropics has some special features, not the least having to do with the climate. Daytime temperatures regularly rise above 90 degrees F every day of the year over most of the country, and in places the humidity stays at virtually 100 percent. High temperatures and humidity are, as a well-meaning Kodak booklet explains, "unfavourable to the life and performance of all sensitized materials and some types of apparatus." By the end of the week some of the photographers were beginning to feel that this might also apply to them, and a steady stream of perspiration onto and into cameras was for many a novel hazard.

In 1869, the renowned Victorian naturalist Alfred Russell Wallace wrote: "Bathed by the tepid water of the great tropical oceans, this region enjoys a climate more uniformly hot and moist than almost any other part of the globe, and teems with natural productions which are elsewhere unknown." By mid-afternoon of the second day, a dozen or so of the less welcome natural productions had lovingly attached themselves to Michael Freeman and his guides as they pushed through a forest trail overlooking the Gaat River in Sarawak. Malaysia hosts several dozen species of leech. Fortunately, this was the (relatively) dry season, and both leeches and mosquitoes were in less than their usual abundance.

In the event, it was haze that emerged as the biggest problem for many of the photographers. It began in mid-August, a blanket settling down over the peninsula and much of Borneo, and was

Left: Abdullah Hamzah, *top right:* CT Fong, *bottom right:* Bernard Hermann

Duangdao

Pisit Jiropas

Georg Gerster

already the focus of controversy by the time the project started. At first, bushfires in northern Australia were blamed, then local pollution was suggested, and the press made it an issue. The project's aerial photographers had an insider's view; from his Alouette helicopter, Georg Gerster could see oil palm factories contributing plumes of smoke. Because Kuala Lumpur lies in a shallow basin, the capital suffered more than most areas, with an inversion layer holding a layer of smoke in place. Over Sarawak, Bernard Hermann spotted crops being burnt off and patches of forest being cleared by fire by Iban farmers: August is in the dry season, and the season for burning. For the photographers it became a special concern at the point where it completely veiled the sun. So much of photography depends on the quality of the light, and when this has been deadened by a flat, grey overcast, the range of possible images is cut right back.

Nevertheless, professional photographers are accustomed to making the best of the available conditions. The project was as much an assignment as any magazine feature story, and at the end of it good pictures were needed, whatever the problems. Also, among so many photographers, not everyone shared the same opinions about what the ideal conditions should be. Ken Duncan, as one of the two specialist landscape photographers, was more at mercy than most to the capricious weather, yet still found ways to make it work for him. "You have to learn to work with the weather, not against it. It's important to get past the blue sky mentality and go with what there is." The typical regime for a landscape photographer revolves around the possibilities of light, and starts with being out on location before dawn.

Duncan's speciality is the panorama, and he works almost exclusively with large-format cameras that produce images between two and three times as long as they are deep. While the equipment is unusual, Duncan uses it to stay as close as possible to the reality of nature: "This is the way we see landscapes — as horizontal views."

Like Duncan, Duangdao Suwanarungsi has a strong attachment to the landscapes that she photographs, and a particular love for mountains, borne out of years of working in the remote areas of her native Thailand. Her particular penance for this was the most physically gruelling assignment of the project, 120km of hiking and climbing up the jungle trails of Gunung Tahan. Although the summit of the 2,178m peak was not the aim of her assignment (despite its height, the mountain's profile is shallow, and there are no clear views from the top), the route up its slopes is tough going. This is no manicured national park for day-trippers, but the reward was an unspoiled and seldom-visited wilderness; "a great challenge but very pure nature," as Duangdao put it.

Her compatriot Pisit Jiropas, with experience of a wide range of tropical landscapes, was assigned to the island of Langkawi. Malaysia's other well-known resort island, Tioman, was entrusted to William Waterfall, whose extensive coverage of his native Hawaii equipped him well to handle its classic beach views. Abdullah Hamzah, meanwhile, was given the difficult task of searching out his speciality — rapids and waterfalls — in the height of the dry season.

While the others could work around the problematic lighting, the four aerial photographers felt that things could hardly have been worse. On the ground there are endless ways of coping with poor light — move indoors, for instance, switch attention to subjects that photograph well without the gloss of attractive lighting, or use flash. In the air there are few such choices. From 600m, the conditions that softened the sunlight for the group portrait that Luca Tettoni shot in Kuala Lumpur made most of Malaysia look as if it were being viewed through the fug of a bar full of chain-smokers. Only from about 100m did most of the landscape become recognisable.

For Georg Gerster, whose latest book on American farmlands from the air was in the process of being published, this was especially frustrating. For the images that he feels capture the full potential of aerial photography, those that reveal structure and

Top left: Duangdao Suwanarungsi, *bottom left:* Pisit Jiropas, *right:* Georg Gerster

function, Gerster is usually compelled to fly relatively high — at 300-600m. For the best part of the week this was impossible, and along with Alberto Cassio, Bernard Hermann and CT Fong, all covering different parts of the country, he had for the most part to fly only a few hundred metres from the ground.

Even within the fairly specialised field of aerial photography, there are differences in style and technique. For everyone, flying time was precious. Refuelling and servicing needs controlled the flight plans, and the RMAF helicopters were limited to five hours a day. Much of this was spent getting to targets, and shooting had to be rapid and efficient. Gerster's solution is to have eight camera bodies all loaded in the aircraft to waste no time loading in flight; Cassio, working with slower and heavier roll-film cameras, flew with an assistant whose sole job was to keep the cameras freshly loaded. One of Cassio's special projects was to photograph Mt Kinabalu, the 4,101m mass of granite — Malaysia's highest mountain — that towers over northern Sabah. The altitude posed its own problem, for the helicopters had an operational ceiling more than a kilometre lower. The view up to the peak from the open door took in the rotor blades; to avoid these in the picture, Cassio worked out a system with the pilot, who would approach, then on a signal bank and turn away. For a few seconds only, the view was clear.

As Cassio's helicopter was performing its complicated manoeuvers over the mountain, wildlife photographer Frans Lanting was searching the tangled cloud forest below for Kinabalu's famous pitcher plants which live on a diet of insects — just one small group of the region's ecological riches. Capturing Malaysia's spectacularly varied natural history was one of the special tasks of the project, and the five photographers assigned to cover it were all experienced naturalists.

Despite the richness of the country's flora and fauna, however, it is one of the most difficult places in the world in which to photograph the real prizes — the large mammals. Tropical rainforest teems with the smaller creatures (116 species of snake, for instance, 1,700 species of parasitic worm, and an entirely unknown number of insects), but few large mammals. Besides,

the whole style of rainforest life is secretive — even the 300kg tapir can slide almost noiselessly through the undergrowth.

The heart of the forest has a cathedral-like gloom. Even at midday, very little light penetrates through the canopy 30-60m above, and the forest floor is typically a hundred times less bright than in full sunlight. The best chances for photographing the larger animals were at the forest edges, such as clearings, watering holes and river banks. Slim Sreedharan, already familiar with the Bako reserve in Sarawak, had had a small lightweight blind specially made in Singapore a few weeks before. Working with a telephoto lens, he set up feeding stations for the birds, and with this technique along the waterline he was able to get shots of sandpipers as close as three metres.

There were disappointments and successes. Karl Ammann and Gerald Cubitt recruited aboriginal Orang Asli trackers in Taman Negara to find tigers. They had known from the start that the odds were against them. Ammann used a technique that he had perfected in Kenya, where he lives: pressure plates concealed along a likely trail and connected electronically to a camera and flash. Checking the camera one morning, he found that 16 frames had been exposed. Unfortunately, nothing had trodden on the plate — the rain had shorted the lead.

In Sabah, however, Jean-Paul Ferrero had had good luck. His guide on the Menanggol River, near Sukau, had found a troop of proboscis monkeys. Shy and rare, they were all but impossible to track in the deep forest, but Ferrero discovered that they returned to the same spot on the river bank each night to sleep. Before dawn, he and his guide paddled silently up-river and moored on the opposite bank. The monkeys began to move around at first light, still too dark for photography, even with the very light-sensitive 7kg telephoto lens that Ferrero was using. Over the course of a couple of days, he found that between the time when the light was bright enough and the

Left: Slim Sreedharan, *right:* Jean-Paul Ferrero

departure of the troop for the day's feeding there was just a 20-minute window of opportunity. He started shooting at 1/15 of a second, holding his breath and waiting for moments when the monkeys were still. Finally, on the second day, Ferrero's patience was rewarded with something special — a pair of the monkeys mating. His film log for the day reads, "Proboscis copulating. Great!!"

Lanting, too, had a reason to celebrate, although his prize subject was completely immobile. One of Kinabalu's oddities is Rafflesia, the world's largest and most massive flower. This bizarre, fleshy and putrid-smelling bloom had been one of Lanting's targets from the start, although the odds were very high against him finding one. The thick petals unfold overnight and begin to rot after only a day or two. They made enquiries through the network of guides and settlements around the mountain, and discovered that workers at the copper mine on the eastern slope had found a small area where Rafflesia occasionally bloomed. To protect the plants, the mine manager had fenced it off discreetly. Lanting's guide showed him how to identify the trailing stems of the grape-vine to which Rafflesia is a parasite, and they combed the steep slope. Quite soon, they found a bud, and then another. Then, in the tangle of undergrowth, the guide caught a glimpse of red marbled with white spots: a freshly bloomed Rafflesia. "We were very lucky indeed," said Lanting later, "but it proved once again how much I need local people in my work. When the pictures are good, the photographer comes out as the hero, but the unsung ones are the local helpers." This became one of the understated themes for the whole project, the part played by the small army of guides, trackers, pilots, boatmen and other helpers. For the photographers, these people were the ground crew, with years of practical experience — the ones who, in Lanting's words, had 'dirt under their fingernails'.

Also in Sabah, but offshore for the week, were two underwater photographers, Tommy Chang and Herwarth Voigtmann. Chang stayed and worked at a pearl farm (and for safety slept there, too, under the

protection of armed guards posted to look out for Filipino pirates). A high plankton build-up at the tail-end of a typhoon had cut visibility down to some 5m, making shark baiting too dangerous. Not only do plankton and other floating particles make the distance appear blurred and hazy, but they have a disastrous effect on flash photography underwater — the light reflects off the particles to create what is known as back-scatter, an effect that looks like an underwater snowstorm. Chang altered his tactics and worked mainly with an extreme wide-angle lens, which allowed him to shoot close to his subjects.

On the west coast, Voigtmann's solution to the poor visibility near the surface was to dive deeper. At Pulau Sipadan he found that the water was clear below a thermocline that varied from 20 to 30m. With a deepest dive of 55m, he was working close to the limit of safety, and was paying close attention to the decompression tables. Too rapid an ascent causes nitrogen to bubble in the bloodstream, and the risk is cumulative from dive to dive.

One of the most impressive locations was a cave system with an entrance at 20m. Accompanied by the owner of the dive lodge, Ron Holland, Voigtmann followed a fixed line 80m into the cave. "By about halfway along I could see the entrance behind as only a slightly less dark patch. At the end, there was no light at all." The darkness was disorienting, and this may have been the explanation for the strangest sight of all — the skeletons of about 20 turtles in a big cave beyond. There was a narrow exit, so narrow that the divers had to pull in their stomachs to squeeze through. "At the mouth there was a ledge, an attractive place for a turtle to sleep. I imagine that

Left: Frans Lanting, *right:* Jean-Paul Ferrero

occasionally a turtle swam in the wrong direction after waking, into the cave, and once there couldn't find the way out in the blackness. It could happen to a diver, too."

A similar thought crossed Noble's mind as the caving team entered the Sarawak Chamber. Three hours into the system and far from any natural light, his moment of disorientation came when they came out of the passage into the chamber and started to walk around the central talus cone, formed by rocks collapsing from above. He asked the guide where exactly they were, and the uncertain reply was, "I'm not sure." The guide had last been this far six years previously.

The Sarawak Chamber topped a week of caving superlatives for Noble. At Deer Cave on the first day they had watched 12 million bats spiralling out into the jungle through the world's largest cave opening (and thankful to see them go, too, for they had spent the afternoon underneath these same bats, which deposit three tons of droppings daily in a steady, stinking rain). This was followed on the second day by Clearwater Cave, part of Southeast Asia's longest system, 12km; and now the largest enclosed space on earth, 600m long, 450m wide and 100m high, bigger even than the Astrodome in Houston, Texas. In Kuching people were fond of explaining its dimensions in terms of the number of Boeing 747s it could house (40 wing-tip to wing-tip), but it was also true, and of more local reference, that it could embrace 350 karaoke bars of average size.

Size and darkness also give cave photography a unique character — flash is essential, but not one only. Noble set up the cameras on a tripod and had other members of the team carry flash units, cueing them to trigger each unit by voice. Including other cavers in the photographs was a deliberate way of conveying scale, which could easily have been lost without a familiar reference (and in the absence of a 747).

Then there were the peoples of Malaysia. Throughout the country, communities of all kinds had their photographer-in-residence for the week, from fishing villages on the east coast to tin-mining camps.

While the specialists were applying esoteric techniques to subjects that ranged from parrot-fish to the contoured patterns of an oil palm plantation from the air, the main topic for most of the photographers was people.

In Malaysia's multi-racial society, the variety of faces and cultures was significant, and the project's second principal theme was this diversity. The country's forests, rivers and coastlines have done much to mould ways of life, but Malaysia is also heir to three of the world's major cultural traditions. Muslim, Chinese and Indian communities here co-exist uniquely, and the country runs very much as a partnership between distinct cultures. The photographers were chosen as much as possible for their familiarity with the different societies.

Perhaps the most classic of all themes in photography is the human condition: daily life seen with a compassionate, understanding eye. People at work, the family, inter-relationships, rites of passage: all these form the raw material for reportage photography. Here, photographic equipment is for the most part less important than observation: an eye for a particular moment in which a gesture, an expression, or a special juxtaposition conveys some aspect of people's lives that strikes a chord in the viewer. Yet within this broad, rich area of photography there is specialisation. There were communities whose lives the editors wanted detailing in depth, while some other locations, such as city streets, would benefit

from a faster, more glancing view. Then, too, certain societies cannot be entered as easily as others. Experienced reportage photographers develop preferences and idiosyncracies, and before the project could begin, the job was to match photographers to assignments — 19 of them for this, the second of the book's three main themes.

Malaysia's spectacular rainforest and mountains are home to distinctive tribal communities, and a team of six photographers was assigned to some of the most remote, forested parts of the country. Until now, so much of the land has remained untouched, particularly in

Left: Karl Ammann, *right:* Hewarth Voightmann

Borneo, that the forest tribes have been able to preserve their traditions for longer than in many other parts of the world. Even so, few of the tribes have been unaffected by the country's social and economic development. For the photographers, all with some anthropological experience, the job was to show societies in transition.

One of the tribes least absorbed into modern Malaysian society is the nomadic Penan, hunter-gatherers who move through the remoter forests of Sarawak in small groups, staying nowhere for longer than a few months. Finding even one group within the week would not be easy. The natural choice for this assignment was Kuching-based Dennis Lau who, since 1968, had been following the elusive Penan. His experience paid off in the Magoh area, where enquiries in one of the settled areas produced reports of a small group somewhere nearby. For three days he and his Penan-speaking guide followed leads and rumours, until one afternoon they came across a clearing with a cluster of thatched shelters. There were only 14 people in the group, and shy. Lau had anticipated this, and had with him copies of photographs that he had taken on previous expeditions. By good fortune, one man recognised a picture of his brother, and the initial barriers of timidity and caution were broken.

To some degree, gaining the confidence of their subjects was a main concern for all the photographers staying with tribal communities. These societies are more closed than most, and photography can sometimes be intrusive. There was a peculiar urgency to be accepted by the longhouse or village quickly enough to start shooting, while observing the customs and social niceties. For Michael Freeman, as for the others, there were few days in which to shoot the Iban longhouse where he was staying on the Gaat river, and this called for fast work on the part of his translator and guides.

Everyone had his own technique for doing this. Around Tasek Cini, near Kuantan, Jean-Noel Reichel devised an unusual, political solution — he brought the democratic process to photography by involving Orang Asli villagers in setting up the pictures. In a Melanau coastal village, John Brunton very much wanted to photograph a curative ceremony performed by one of only two shamans remaining in the community, but not only are the Melanau very reserved, such rituals are taken too seriously to demonstrate merely for the camera. Fortunately, a previous dinner of raw fish came to Brunton's rescue; he was so ill the next day that he actually needed a shamanistic cure, which required that an image of a spirit be carved in an appropriate stance, here clutching its stomach.

For Rio Helmi, the need to get settled in quite quickly was compounded by the travelling time involved. On his way to the Kayan and Kenyah settlements in the heart of Borneo, he logged in 20 hours by boat and five hours on foot — and with the rivers at their lowest for the year, both forms of transport were often combined. Hauling boats up rapids enriched the week's experiences but became yet another hazard for film and cameras. Keeping them out of the sun was already a chore; protecting them from river water demanded even more attention. Helmi, like most of the photographers, found that he was spending much of his time just baby-sitting the equipment, moving it from one patch of shade to another, swaddling it in tarpaulins and making daily inspections for fungus and corrosion.

Mike Yamashita's Kelabit village at Bareo was too far to reach overland in the time available, and he was flown in by helicopter to the mountains bordering Kalimantan. The village lay in a bowl green with paddy rice, "a Shangri-La" to Yamashita. The end-of-planting celebrations were starting as he arrived, and by the end of the first day he had shot 40 rolls. Work was slower on the remaining days, as Yamashita faced the problem of dark interiors common to most of the photographers in tribal villages. One of his solutions was to use an American lighting innovation: a set of miniature flash units strategically placed behind pots, pillars and shelves, all triggered simultaneously by remote control.

Top left: Michael Freeman, *centre left:* Dennis Lau, *bottom left:* Rio Helmi, *right:* Mike Yamashita

Gueorgui Pinkhassov

Abbas

Certainly, many of the locations were chosen for their special character, but in the end, it was the differences in photographic style and technique that produced the variety and vitality in the picture coverage. In the specialised fields of underwater, landscape, wildlife, and so on, technique is easy to pinpoint. In reportage, it is more elusive to define, but no less important. One traditional precept is to observe without altering the way people behave — 'minimum intrusion' as Ian Berry describes it. To achieve this is no easy matter, and particularly in a society where most of the photographers looked so obviously foreign.

"Ideally," said Richard Kalvar, "I'd like to be on the edges but at the same time penetrate, but it was obviously more difficult for me to blend in here in Malay villages than in a European city. And for my own part I don't like pictures in which people are looking at the camera." Nevertheless, working with a wide-angle lens, for example, it was often possible for Kalvar to get candid images close to people, who did not realise how much of the view the photographer could see. Kalvar, like Bruno Barbey, covered part of the traditional northeast of the peninsula.

Abbas, assigned to kampongs in Prai and continuing his long-running coverage of Islamic societies, disagreed with the view that more time spent on the assignment would have helped. "You can often get the essence of things almost instantly, with luck and preparation. What is important is your own disposition. If you are ready and open, things happen to you. When you shut off, things close down." True to the principle of creating one's own luck, Abbas noticed a sign in Arabic on the wall of a mosque on the last day, and asked for a translation. It announced a marriage — for the next day. He stayed on, got himself invited, and had the best photographic situation of his week. Like Berry, Kalvar and several other reportage photographers, he favours quiet, uncomplicated cameras, and a few lenses only, carrying the minimum so as to be as mobile as possible.

An additional streamlining is to use just one kind of film, so as to reduce confusion and save time in changing film speed settings. Just as Abbas was a natural choice for the Islamic side of Malaysian life, so Patrick Zachmann was ideal for Chinese communities in Ipoh — he has for some years now been working on a project to record Chinese society around the world. Ipoh was particularly appropriate, for it was to the tin industry here that the main influx of the Chinese population arrived around the turn of the century. A similar historical connection directed Steve McCurry's assignment to Indian communities working rubber plantations. McCurry himself was familiar with the region through an earlier lengthy assignment, and book, on the monsoon.

The maritime influence on Malaysian life has always been strong. The country's position between the South China, Andaman and Java seas is not only responsible for the movements of people that have created the unique ethnic mix, but has also given it a sea-faring tradition. Three of the photographers, each with experience of living with fishing communities, were assigned to coastal villages — Jean Gaumy, who has a long-term project underway on man and the sea, Pierre Argo from Mauritius, and Kazuyoshi Nomachi, whose book on the Nile has won wide acclaim.

As everywhere, cities offer a sharp contrast with rural traditions, and the pace of life in Kuala Lumpur demanded a very different approach. This is Paul Chesley's speciality, and capturing the atmosphere of energy and vitality in a city kept him working long hours: there was no shortage of locations and events. The principal event of the week, which had been a factor in timing the entire project, was the National Day parade. Chesley shot this from all angles, including the roof of one high-rise building where he unwittingly left a trail of footprints for posterity in the newly laid surface of tar. Escaping the wrath of the janitor added an urgency to his already frenetic schedule.

Georgui Pinkhassov's highly

Paul Chesley

Steve McCurry

Top left: Abbas, *bottom left:* Georgui Pinkhassov, *top right:* Paul Chesley, *bottom right:* Steve McCurry

Basil Pao

Dominic Sansoni

unusual style of street photography was put to work in Penang. His use of high-speed film and deliberate choice of strangely and dimly lit scenes was well-suited to a night-time view of street markets and alleyways in the Chinatown of this old port, while his unconventional compositions brought a refreshing perspective to the book's photography. Pinkhassov's approach demonstrates very well just how stylistic differences between photographers play a considerable role in making images distinctive. These differences go beyond just technique — the way of reaching a particular picture — and reflect conflicting opinions about what photography should or can do.

For instance, Berry's views about not intruding on a situation are shared by a number of reportage photographers. However, with the scope of the book being an entire country, straight reportage photography can only go a certain distance in portraying life and culture. From the start, the editors had been faced with the challenge of portraying *all* aspects of Malaysian culture — more than could be found by photojournalists in off-the-cuff situations. An important part of any culture is expressed through traditions which occupy a special rather than an everyday part of life, and these traditions formed the third theme of the book's photography. Whether in the form of folk art, ceremonies or architecture, they called for advance organisation, and for a number of photographers whose specialities lay in being able to plan, direct and, above all, create images.

Dominic Sansoni's speciality, for instance, is his eye for graphic detail, and on this project he was given the opportunity to bring it to bear on a subject that was particularly appropriate for him — Malacca. Its rich history and unusual architectural mix stems from an amalgam of Malay, Portuguese and Dutch cultures; Sansoni himself is from a third generation Burgher community in Sri Lanka, and was at home in this kind of overlay of traditions.

Leonard Lueras, while assigned to an Iban longhouse, focused on textiles rather than everyday life. He was fortunate enough to be accompanied to his Iban longhouse by a friend who had spent years there studying the subject. Having just completed a book on tribal art in Borneo, Lueras already had a special interest in Iban weaving and its role in the culture.

For a number of photographers, their assignments specifically called for control and organisation. Gerald Gay, for instance, brought his studio experience to bear on food in Penang. Steve Vidler's style of shooting was admirably suited to the performing arts in Kelantan. Top-spinning, kites, drumming and village theatre are no longer everyday occurrences; indeed, August was not even the season for kite-flying. Nevertheless, Vidler had a clear idea in advance of how he needed to organise things so as to yield strong images and arranged a series of special performances throughout this northeastern state.

Nik Wheeler, with a roving assignment in Sabah, also had performances to shoot — in particular a Murut dance on a specially sprung floor. This sunken platform of tethered bamboo trunks gave a natural bounce, which the Muruts use for a trampoline-like dance, and which required Wheeler to climb up to the roof and hang precariously from the timbers for his overhead shot. In Sabah at the same time as Wheeler was Ara Guler from Turkey, bringing his ethnographic experience to bear on Kadazan communities.

Basil Pao's method in covering Chinese culture in Penang at the time of the Hungry Ghost Festival was to get involved, with the help of his guides. However, as this also included certain dealings with the spirit world, he found that on one occasion he came a little too close for comfort to the supernatural. The problem arose when he tried to photograph a medium in trance. The procedure took some effort and time on the part of the medium, but each time he entered the trance, Pao's flash unit seized up. As

Nik Wheeler

Top left: Georgui Pinkhassov, *bottom left:* Dominic Sansoni, *right:* Nik Wheeler the medium came out into the real world, so the flash began working again. To compound Pao's frustration, the next day it slipped from his fingers — not once, but three times, finally smashing completely. Commented the normally sceptical Pao: "I learned that spirits don't like strobes."

Raghu Rai was the natural choice for the cultural aspects of Indian society. A firm believer in Henri Cartier-Bresson's dictum 'the decisive moment' — and indeed, a disciple of Cartier-Bresson, Rai's style of shooting is exemplified by his picture of silhouetted dancers. Also in Kuala Lumpur, Rene Burri, who has long experience in photographing the powerful and famous, was recruited for a different stratum of society. His crucial assignment was the Royal Palace, which included a portrait of Malaysia's King and Queen.

Paul Chesley

Nicholas DeVore's style was different again from all these. Self-proclaimed "unorthodox and non-conventional", DeVore nowadays dresses to attract attention. On his roving assignment around Negri Sembilan, he found that this made people take more of an outgoing interest in what he was doing. "I think they thought I was more of a spectacle than I thought they were." His interest lay not in detail and content, but in "blurred, impressionistic interpretations of colour, form and movement", and to this end he used a range of techniques that he has perfected over the years since he left 'straight' reportage photography. "I use slow shutter speeds, pans, soft focus 'huffers', and seldom a tripod. If I can't get it sharp, I'll blur it." DeVore's "huffers" are exactly what they sound like — breathing condensation on the front of the lens to make a customised filter. Another invention is altered focus. Making a double exposure through a window spattered with raindrops, DeVore focused first on the scene beyond, then on the drops on the pane. The result is a picture with all normal ingredients, but an oddness that is hard to place without being privy to the technique.

Michelangelo Durazzo's style has been influenced by his long association with Ernst Haas who, more than anyone else, was responsible for creating a photographic version of impressionism. Assistant to Haas for many years, Durazzo's feeling for the play of light and for colour were directed towards his favourite subjects — architecture and the plastic arts — in and around Kuala Lumpur. By the weekend, September 1, the photographers were making their way to Kuching where the film would be collected and the debriefings would take place. The quantities of film shot reflected the variety of assignments, and ranged from 19 rolls to 129.

O n the last day, 2,850 rolls of film lay packed in plastic bags on the floor of the operations room in the Kuching Hilton. Until it reached the laboratories in Kuala Lumpur and Tokyo, the entire book lay in undeveloped emulsion, a fragile state of uncertainty for a project of such a scale. Chief Photographer Luca Tettoni stood looking at it reflectively, wondering how well all the assignments had gone. The debriefings on this kind of project only occasionally gave a clue. At best you knew who had been where and done what. Beyond that there was no way of telling where in all that mass of film lay the special images — the pictures that would catch the eye and the mind. The photographers themselves were usually reticent about the shots that they expected to be good, and hopeful about the uncertain ones. This was really the moment beyond which nothing could be added. The way that Malaysia looked for this one week was now irrevocably sealed, and pleasantly beyond the control of anyone but the editors of the book.

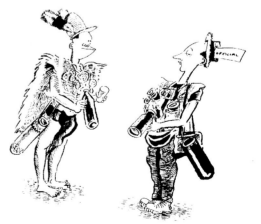

Left: René Burri, *top right:* Michelangelo Durazzo, *bottom right:* Nicholas DeVore

MALAYSIA

ABDULLAH HAMZAH, *Kuala Lumpur*
His love of shooting nature has led Abdullah (43) to roam all over the country in search of the perfect photograph in his favourite 120 format. A photographer for the Tourist Development Corp for many years, his latest book is *Waterfalls of Malaysia*.

TOMMY CHANG, *Kota Kinabalu*
Having been a diver for more than 10 years, Chang (40) specialises in underwater photography. Freelancing since 1983 after he quit the film unit of Radio Television Malaysia-Sabah – where he was a photographer, cameraman and film editor – Chang has worked with advertising agencies, travel magazine and book publishers.

C.T. FONG, *Penang*
A professional photographer for more than 13 years, Fong (34) started out as a newspaper photographer. He now specialises in advertising, travel and nature photography. He has published a number of books, including *Langkawi: Legends in the Paradise* and *Penang: Splendour and Wonders*.

DENNIS LAU, *Kuching*
Born and raised in Sarawak, Lau (53) started taking pictures at the age of 13. A teacher by profession, his intimate knowledge of Sarawak has enabled him to put together a unique photographic record of the environment and its peoples, in particular the nomadic Penan.

SLIM SREEDHARAN, *Kuala Lumpur*
A specialist in wildlife photography, Sreedharan (50) is a former journalist and ornithologist who has worked on conservation projects in Africa, India and Southeast Asia with the Worldwide Fund for Nature and other similar bodies. Now concentrating on documentary films linked to conservation, he has published four books – *Bako, A Living Museum; Humble Beginnings; Caught in a Muddle* and *Snakes and Ladders*.

ASIA

DUANGDAO SUWANARUNGSI, *Thailand*
Following her personal interests in nature and conservation, Duangdao (36) has become her country's pre-eminent landscape photographer. A photographer for the Tourist Authority of Thailand, she has published several books of her work, including *Back to the Mountain* and *7 Days in the Kingdom*.

KEN DUNCAN, *Australia*
A specialist in panoramic landscapes which he has been shooting since 1982 in his native Australia, Duncan (40) uses medium-format camera equipment that produces images between two and three times as long as they are deep.

GERALD GAY, *Singapore*
Returning to his native Singapore from Melbourne in 1984 after five years, Gay (33) does advertising and corporate photography, specialising in fashion, food, interiors and architecture. He set up Developing Agents agency in 1986.

RIO HELMI, *Indonesia*
Bali-based Helmi (37) was chief photographer for *Indonesia: A Voyage Through The Archipelago*. A former editor of the *Sunday Bali Post* and associate editor of *Mutiara* magazine, he went freelance in 1983. His work has appeared in many books on Bali as well as in Indonesian, Japanese, French and German magazines. He recently produced a book on the Mahakam River of East Kalimantan.

KAZUYOSHI NOMACHI, *Japan*
A student of the famous Japanese photographer Takashi Kijima, Nomachi (45) is the author of eight books of photographs and essays, including *Sahara* and *The Nile*. Winner of numerous photographic awards, his work has appeared in *Life*, *Stern* and *National Geographic*.

BASIL PAO, *Hong Kong*
Starting his extensive career in New York in 1973, Pao (38) worked in Hong Kong, Los Angeles and New York as a designer, art director, writer and producer before deciding to concentrate on photography in 1986. His pictures – in particular those he shot on the set of *The Last Emperor* where he worked as assistant director – have been widely used in US and Asian magazines.

PISIT JIROPAS, *Thailand*
A painter until 12 years ago, Pisit (45) studied art in Silapakorn University, Bangkok. He worked on a similar assignment to this book in his native Thailand and was also involved in the photography of *Singapore: Island City State*.

RAGHU RAI, *India*
India's foremost photographer for the past 25 years, Raghu (59) recently documented the way of life of the Dalai Lama and his people in *Tibet In Exile*. Widely published and exhibited, twenty-five of his photographs are held in the permanent collection of the Bibliothéque Nationale in Paris.

DOMINIC SANSONI, *Sri Lanka*
After studying art in England, Sansoni (35) has become more involved in news and war photography in his homeland in recent years, working for a variety of international news and feature magazines. He has published several books on travel and documentary subjects.

EUROPE

ABBAS, *France/Iran*
A magazine reportage photographer since the late 1960s, Abbas (46) – a Magnum photographer – has covered a wide range of political subjects and areas of conflict, including Biafra, Vietnam and the Middle East. An Iranian and a Muslim, he has a particularly strong interest in Islamic subjects.

KARL AMMANN, *Switzerland/Kenya*
A former hotelier who developed a passion for photography, Ammann (43) is now resident in Nairobi, where his pictures of African wildlife have been published as books, including *Cheetah* in 1984, followed by *The Hunter and the Hunted* (1988) and *Masai Mara* (1990).

PIERRE ARGO, *France/Mauritius*
A magazine reportage photographer, Argo (49) has worked in the Indian Ocean region and published two books on Mauritius. Paris-based since 1981, he is working on two books on the Seychelles.

BRUNO BARBEY, *France*
Born in Morocco, Paris-based Barbey (50) is a member of Magnum. Since the early 1960s, he has worked on assignments throughout the world for *Life*, *Stern*, *National Geographic*, *Geo*, *Paris-Match* and *The Sunday Times*. A winner of many prestigious awards, his work has been exhibited in Paris, London, Rome and Zurich.

IAN BERRY, *London, England*
A social documentary photographer, Berry (57) began his career with the African *Drum* magazine in 1953. Working for the *Observer* magazine through the 1960s and a member of Magnum since 1961, he has worked in Africa (including the Congo and Sharpeville); the Far East, the Middle East and Europe.

JOHN BRUNTON, *England/France*
After graduating from the London School of Economics, Brunton (35) moved into advertising, which brought him to Malaysia in 1982. Captured by the spell of the Orient, this Paris-based Briton has travelled extensively in Southeast Asia. Describing himself as "completely untrained", his work has appeared in *Elle*, *Life* and *Geo* as well as leading British newspapers. He plans to publish a book of photographs of rural France.

RENE BURRI, *Zurich, Switzerland*
A full member of Magnum since 1959, Burri (58) received the International Film and Television Award in New York in 1967 in recognition of his long association with film. Elected European vice-president of Magnum in 1982, his work is published in major books and exhibition catalogues.

ALBERTO CASSIO, *Italy/Thailand*
Bangkok-based Cassio (43) is one of Thailand's best-known photographers. A specialist in aerial photography, he has published a number of books, including a view of Thailand from the air with Luca Tettoni.

GERALD CUBITT, *England/Africa*
A freelance photographer specialising in wildlife and natural history pictures, Cubitt (52) has worked extensively in East, Central and southern Africa over the past 20 years. He has published 15 books including *Wild Malaysia* in 1991, and operates a photolibrary with outlets throughout the world.

MICHELANGELO DURAZZO, *Italy/France*
Born in Rome, Paris-based Durazzo (56) was previously

assistant to both Ernst Haas and Brian Brake. A former member of Magnum, Durazzo now produces books and photographs for magazines, specialising in theatre, the arts and architecture.

JEAN PAUL FERRERO,
France/Australia
Turning a childhood interest in animals into a career as a wildlife photographer, Paris-born Ferrero (40) travelled constantly on magazine assignments for almost 10 years before settling in Australia in 1982 to concentrate on the continent's landscape and wildlife, as well as those of New Zealand, Papua New Guinea and Antartica.

MICHAEL FREEMAN,
London, England
An editorial photographer since 1973, Freeman (46) travels several months a year from his London home. *The Smithsonian's* contract photographer, he specialises in travel reportage, chiefly in Asia, and scientific special effects. He has written many books on photography, his most recent book is *Angkor: The Hidden Glories.*

JEAN GAUMY, *Paris, France*
A member of Magnum since 1986, Gaumy (33) has also directed two French films. A photographer since his undergraduate days in Rouen, France, he was the first to document French prison life. He has travelled extensively in Central America and Iran and has published a few books.

GEORG GERSTER,
Zurich, Switzerland
Swiss doyen of aerial photographers, Gerster (63) continues to live near Zurich. A specialist in aerial photography, for nearly 30 years, he has published many books and is represented in many permanent collections.

His 1976 book *The Grand Design* (*Der Mensch auf Seiner Erde*) is a classic of the genre.

ARA GULER, *Turkey*
Istanbul-based Guler (63) has documented his country in magazines and books. He has worked for *Life*, *Paris-Match* and *Stern* magazines and continues on assignments in Europe and America. In 1984, he published a book on his 25 years' work on famous people, archaeology and popular art.

BERNARD HERMANN,
Paris, France
Starting his career as a newspaper photographer in Paris, Hermann (50) then went to work with Gamma agency. From 1971 on, he worked with *Les Editions du Pacifique*, Times Editions in publishing a series on islands, then on cities including San Francisco, New York, Paris, Rio de Janeiro, London, New Orleans and Honolulu.

FRANS LANTING, *Holland/USA*
After moving to the US in 1978, Lanting (40) began his photographic career in 1980, going on to work for *Geo* in 1982 and *National Geographic* in 1985. Best known for his wildlife photography, in the last few years he has been on assignments in locations from the Antarctic to African swamps. He has several books to his name, including *Madagascar: A World Out of Time*.

GUEORGUI PINKHASSOV,
USSR/France
An assistant in Moscow's Mossfilm Studios until 1985, Pinkhassov (39) became an independent photojournalist for a number of magazines before moving to Paris where he became a member of Magnum in 1988. He was also on the photographic team of *Indonesia: A Voyage through the Archipelago*.

JEAN-NOEL REICHEL,
Paris, France
A photo-journalist after finishing his graphic arts studies, Reichel (42) spent 10 years travelling round the world documenting cultures for the French press group, *Réalities Hachette*. He is now one of France's foremost advertising photographers.

LUCA INVERNIZZI TETTONI,
Italy/Thailand
Before re-locating in Bangkok, Tettoni (42) worked in Indonesia for several years, having left Italy in 1978. Although annual reports and advertising are his main line of work, his first love as a photographer remains sculpture and archaeology, for which his work in South and Southeast Asia is well known. He was one of the winners of the 1985 PATA awards for his contribution to the promotion of Southeast Asia.

STEVE VIDLER, *England/Japan*
Describing himself as a complete nomad, Vidler (42) has been travelling for the past 26 years and claims the world as his studio. Before becoming a photographer, he worked in some 50 different jobs in as many countries. Today he is one of the most successful and prolific independent travel photographers in the world.

HERWARTH VOIGTMANN,
Germany/Maldives
An underwater specialist who started his own scuba-diving school on the Salerne Gulf in 1971, Voigtmann (54) has won international recognition as a pioneer, particularly for his spectacular pictures on sharks.

NIK WHEELER, *London, England*
Named 'Travel Photographer of the Year' in 1988, Wheeler (52) shoots regularly for *Time*, *Life*, *Newsweek*, *Geo* and *National Geographic*. His books include *The Insider's Guide to Japan* and *This is China*. He lives in Los Angeles.

PATRICK ZACHMANN,
Paris, France
A regular contributor of periodicals such as *Actuel*, *Geo* and *Liberation*, Zachmann (36) had a travelling exhibition of his photo reportage on the Mafia in Naples in 1982. Since 1987, he has been working on the Chinese diaspora for a book, *The Eye of a Long Nose*. Recipient of the Niepce Award in 1989, he became a member of Magnum in 1990.

USA

PAUL CHESLEY, *Aspen, Colorado*
Having participated in ten *Day in the Life* projects, Chesley has travelled throughout Japan, Europe, South America, the United States and Australia. Exhibitions of his work have been held in the US and Japan and his pictures can be seen in *National Geographic*, *Fortune*, *Geo*, *The Smithsonian* and *Esquire* magazines.

NICHOLAS DEVORE III, *Aspen, Colorado*
Paris-born Devore (42) worked as a forest ranger before becoming a *National Geographic* photographer. More recently, he has changed direction from straight reportage to a more personal, expressive style.

RICHARD KALVAR, *Paris, France*
New York-born Kalvar (46) moved to Paris in 1970 and is a member of Magnum. He specialises in street photography and has worked on assignments in Europe and America. Since the 1980s, he has been working more in Asia. He is also working on a long-term black and white project in Rome.

LEONARD LUERAS, *Bali, Indonesia*
A writer-photographer-editor-designer-publisher of some 50 books, mostly about travel and culture, Lueras (46) is at present

resident in Bali where he is creative director of Image Network Indonesia. Born in New Mexico and raised in Southern California, he has lived in the Asia-Pacific region since 1963, when he first went to Hawaii and fell in love with surfing.

STEVE McCURRY, *New York, New York*
Best known for his photographic work on India, McCurry (41) has won several prestigious awards for his reportages including the Robert Capa Gold Medal awarded by the Overseas Press Club for his coverage of Afghanistan in 1980. He has published a number of books, including *Monsoon* and *The Imperial Way*.

CHRIS NOBLE, *Salt Lake City, Utah*
A love of adventure combined with writing and photography, has given Noble (36) a career which provides assignments in the most beautiful and remote areas of the world, including the Himalayas and in Alaska. His work appears regularly in specialist outdoor magazines as well as in *Life*, *Geo* and *National Geographic*.

WILLIAM WATERFALL, *Honolulu, Hawaii*
Owner of one of the strongest stock files on the Hawaiian islands, Waterfall (43) has his pictures appearing regularly in *Islands*, *The New York Times*, *The New Yorker*, *National Geographic* and *Traveller* as well as many books on Hawaii.

MIKE YAMASHITA, *Paramus, New Jersey*
Featured regularly in *National Geographic* and *Time*, Yamashita (42) also travels all over the world for Nikon, Singapore Airlines and Diners Club. He did *Lakes, Peaks and Prairies: Discovering the US-Canadian Border* in 1984.

Kodak the world leader in photography is represented in Malaysia by Kodak (Malaysia) Sdn Bhd. Established in 1952, it provides quality photographic products and services to the consumer, finisher, professionals, motion picture, presentation techniques, graphic arts, business imaging and health science markets.

Malaysia Airlines or MAS, . established in 1972 as Malaysia's flag carrier, currently flies to 49 international and 35 domestic destinations. It operates a fleet of 60 aircraft including the latest B747-400. Its aircraft maintenance facilities and training simulators are among the most advanced in the region. MAS was recently awarded the AIM/ Executive World Digest 1990 Management Award for excellence in the general management category and the Tourist Development Corporation's coveted Gold Tourism Award the Most Outstanding Contribution to Tourism (Private Sector).

MBf Finance Berhad is committed to servicing people not only in urban centres but also in small towns, thus helping to meet the financial needs of individuals, petty traders, industrialists and developers throughout Malaysia. Such total commitment is integral to the company's philosophy. Placing high priority on the development of human resources, MBf Finance has a qualified and innovative team and with its experience, wide range of financial services and, most important of all, its commitment, touches the lives of a large proportion of the population.

The MUI Group

The MUI Group, since its inception in 1960, has become one of Malaysia's largest business conglomerates. Its highly diversified activities include banking, finance, leasing, insurance, hotel operations, properties, cement manufacturing, trading, news media and international investments. The Group's business operations have extended beyond Malaysia to Singapore, Hongkong, Australia, the United States, Canada and the United Kingdom.

Perusahaan Otomobil Nasional Berhad

PROTON (Perusahaan Otomobil Nasional Berhad), manufacturer of the Malaysian car, Proton Saga, was established as one of the vehicles in the nation's progress towards industrial development. Providing impetus in the quest for technological advancement, primarily in the automobile manufacturing industry, PROTON is proud to have lived up to its promise of delivering quality cars with the hallmark of excellence – a task it will continue to perform.

SPORTS TOTO MALAYSIA

Sports Toto Malaysia Bhd, formed in 1969 to raise funds to promote and develop sports and cultural activities, operates a system of pool betting through Toto games in Malaysia which has grown into a profitable multi-million dollar business. A sponsor of major sports and cultural events and a responsible corporate citizen, the company consistently helps the poor and needy and also supports nation-building projects. Sports Toto is a subsidiary of Berjaya Corp (M) Berhad, itself a subsidiary of Inter-Pacific Industrial Group Berhad.

the Regent
KUALA LUMPUR

The Regent of Kuala Lumpur, in the heart of the Garden City of Lights, is the choice of discerning business travellers – it has a 24-hour business centre. All 469 luxurious rooms and suites are equipped with a two-line IDD facility and provided with butler service. It has five restaurants, eight banquet and meeting rooms and recreational facilities including a health club and an outdoor pool.

United Engineers (Malaysia) Berhad, is responsible for the construction and maintenance of the North-South Expressway, the new Klang Valley Expressway as well as improvements to the Federal Highway Route 2. It also provides project management and consultancy, mechanical, civil engineering and soil investigation services. The company is further involved in the oil and gas industries, electronic communications equipment, transportation, sale of trucks, tyre retreading and vehicle servicing.

SINCE 1955

YTL Corporation Berhad, the flagship of the YTL Group of Companies, established its major subsidiary, Syarikat Pembenaan Yeoh Tiong Lay, in 1955. Over the past 35 years, success and prestige has allowed the company to develop into a major diversified publicly-listed corporation in the construction field. YTL Corporation Berhad has consolidated its position as a leading construction, civil engineering, hotel development and manufacturing group.

AMC

AMC-Melewar Zecha Communications, simply known as AMC, is Malaysia's No. 1 advertising agency, employing about 120 people. Its clients include Malaysia Airlines and the Tourist Development Corporation of Malaysia. Established in late 1976 as a joint venture between The Melewar Corp Berhad, one of Malaysia's leading Bumiputra investment holding companies, and Zecha Holdings Ltd of Hongkong, its involvement with this book commemorates its 15th anniversary in 1991.

Bank Bumiputra Malaysia Berhad, a major commercial bank in Malaysia and one of the largest in Southeast Asia, was incorporated on October 1st 1965 and commenced operations on February 1st 1966. As one of banking's market leaders in Malaysia, with M$2 billion authorised capital and M$1.15 billion paid up, Bank Bumiputra provides a complete range of wholesale and retail banking services through its network of domestic and overseas branches as well as subsidiaries, affiliates and correspondents in all principal cities worldwide.

BYG

Bukit Young Goldmine Sendirian Berhad, owned and operated by Tan Sri Datuk Amar Ling Beng Siew's Group of Companies, is the only modern hard rock gold mine in Malaysia. The modern hydro-metallurgical process used by the company to extract the submicroscopic gold has revolutionised, revived and opened up a new frontier in gold mining in Sarawak.

Esso's upstream company, Esso Production Malaysia Inc, is engaged in the exploration and production of oil and natural gas. It is Malaysia's largest crude oil producer, with a production level of about 320,000 barrels of oil a day and operates 26 platforms offshore Trengganu. Its principal downstream company, Esso Malaysia Berhad, refines 50,000 barrels of oil a day at its Port Dickson refinery. It also markets petroleum products through 336 service stations and more than 700 independent dealers and distributors throughout Malaysia.

The GEC-Marconi companies in Malaysia – among the oldest in the engineering field to be associated closely with the nation's progress and development – supply equipment and technical support services for development and infrastructure projects including power generation, transmission, telecommunications, transportation, defence electronics, medical and health care and consumer electronics. Extensive research and development facilities and engineering services are provided throughout the country through an efficient nationwide network for marketing and technical support services.

Globe Silk Store

Globe Silk Store, one of Malaysia's largest departmental stores and owned by Tan Sri TJ Kishu, was founded in 1930 in Segamat, Johor, by his late father Mr Tirathdas Jethanand. Today, Globe is a household name, located on Jalan Tuanku Abdul Rahman, Kuala Lumpur, in a modern 10-storey building. Globe celebrated its Diamond Jubilee last year and continues to practise its philosophy of providing the customer quality, variety and value for money.

Golden Hope

Golden Hope Plantations Berhad, almost a century old, has become a leader in the Malaysian plantations industry. It owns and manages more than 150,000 hectares of oil palm, rubber, cocoa, coconut and fruit. Its principal activities include operation of estates, fruit cultivation, palm oil refining, manufacture of rubber and coconut-based food products, agricultural and computer consultancy, property development and production of methylesters, refined glycerine and agricultural products.

K U C H I N G

The Kuching Hilton – located in the heart of Kuching, the gateway to Sarawak in legendary Borneo, one of the world's oldest rainforests – has 322 elegantly appointed rooms and suites and three executive floors. Its restaurant and a bar lounge offer an excellent choice of cuisine and entertainment. Extensive facilities for conventions, seminars and meetings are available. The 15-storey main hotel block has a podium which holds the swimming pool, tennis court and a tropical landscaped garden. A fitness centre which has the latest gymnastic equipment offers facilities for sauna, jacuzzi and massage.

IGB Corporation Berhad

IGB Corporation Berhad was incorporated in 1964 and operated initially as a modest

developer of homes in Ipoh, Perak. Today IGB is a publicly listed company in Malaysia with interests in international property development, construction, hotels, manufacturing and trading activities. Having refocused on the Malaysian property scene, IGB is emerging as one of Malaysia's leading developers with a significant role in building the Malaysia of tomorrow.

Magnum Corp Bhd, incorporated in December 1968 and listed on the Kuala Lumpur Stock Exchange in May 1970, operates a licensed 4-digit forecast betting game, a licensed finance company, a holiday resort and tourist complex, property and general investment. It has paid up capital of M$127 million with market capitalisation exceeding M$826 million as at the end of November 1990.

Malaysia LNG Sdn Bhd is a joint venture between PETRONAS (Malaysia's National Oil Company), Shell International, Mitsubishi Corp of Japan and the Sarawak State Government. It operates a US$1.5 billion LNG plant in Bintulu, Sarawak. The three-module plant started operating in 1983. It has a capacity of 8 million tonnes of LNG and sells its products to Japan.

The Malaysia Mining Corp Bhd Group, which prospects for base and precious metals and minerals in Malaysia and overseas, is also one of the world's largest integrated mining establishments, with strategic interests in diamond and gold mining in Australia. It has an established

network covering tin, minerals and other commodities and proven capabilities in engineering and construction.

Malaysia National Insurance Sdn Berhad, incorporated on April 28th 1970, is Malaysia's largest insurance company with total assets at March 31st 1990 of M$1.4 billion and shareholders' funds at M$125 million. It underwrites all classes of general insurance including Fire, Accident, Marine, Aviation and Engineering while in life insurance the company offers a wide range of policies to suit the requirements of the individual or corporate client.

The New Straits Times Press (M) Bhd is the largest newspaper and magazine publisher in Malaysia. The Group's principal activities include publishing Malaysia's leading newspapers, periodicals and books; marketing, supply and provision of data processing equipment and related services, provision of viewdata services via electronic media; wholesaling and retailing of publications and stationery, underwriting of general insurance, and investment holding.

Resorts World Bhd, the premier resort group in Malaysia, owns Genting Highlands Resort, the country's most established tourist destination just 58 km from Kuala Lumpur. Incorporated in 1980, it acquired from its holding company, Genting Bhd, the gaming hotel and resort-related operations of the group in 1989. Its principal activities are gaming, hotels, restaurants, recreation and amusement, golf, country club and condotel operations, property

investment and providing utilities services. Listed on the Kuala Lumpur Stock Exchange in December 1989, Resorts World's M$3.5 billion market capitalisation makes it one of Malaysia's top five companies.

The Sapura Group employs over 2,800 people and has been involved in telecommunications for the past 15 years. Its main activities include manufacturing of telephone sets, public payphones, PABXs, power and telecommunication cables, metal products and automative parts. It also operates public payphones and provides paging services as well as project consultancy, planning, design and installation of telephone cables and optical fibre systems. Its products include the marketing and distribution of telephone terminals, large PABX systems, computers, mobile cellular phones, facsimile machines, keyphones and exports of Sapura designed and manufactured telephone equipment. The Group has its own research and development facility.

Sime Darby Berhad, founded in 1910 by William Middleton Sime and Henry Darby to manage 500 acres of rubber estates, is Southeast Asia's foremost multinational today. It has successfully diversified into other areas, with core business activities in plantations, manufacturing and trading, heavy equipment and motor vehicle distribution and assembly, property development, insurance and the oil and gas industry.

The Lion Group is one of the most diversified and forward-looking companies in the region, its

flagship company being the Amalgamated Steel Mills Bhd. It is also Malaysia's largest retailer through the Parkson chain. It is involved in manufacturing, trading, retailing, finance, property and construction, plantations and agriculture, aquaculture and mixed farming.

DHL, is credited as having launched the international air express industry in 1969, when it delivered vital business documents by air across the Pacific. Today, DHL is the world's largest air express network with more than 24,000 dedicated staff manning more than 1,350 offices in 187 countries.

Far East Offset & Engraving Sdn Bhd, one of the region's leaders in colour separation, services international publishers, printers, advertising agencies and design houses in the United States, Western Europe, Australia and in Malaysia. With its state-of-the-art technology it has a well-earned reputation for consistent high quality work and efficient service for its clients.

Sarawak's Ministry of Environment and Tourism, established in 1986, aims to contribute to the diversification and growth of the State's economy, generate employment and promote national integration through tourism. To do this, the Ministry places priority in improving accessibility and promoting Sarawak as a holiday destination and ensuring that tourism products, infrastructure, facilities and services are adequate and of an acceptable standard.

ACKNOWLEDGEMENTS

IT WOULD HAVE BEEN IMPOSSIBLE TO PRODUCE THIS BOOK WITHOUT THE KIND ASSISTANCE AND SUPPORT OF THE VERY MANY INDIVIDUALS WHO SO GENEROUSLY VOLUNTEERED THEIR TIME, ENERGY AND RESOURCES TO ENSURE THE SMOOTH RUNNING OF THIS PROJECT. THE PUBLISHERS AND PROJECT TEAM ARE FOREVER INDEBTED TO: **DATUK SABARUDDIN CHIK**, MINISTER OF CULTURE, ARTS AND TOURISM FOR THE SUPPORT OF HIS MINISTRY; **DATUK NAPSIAH OMAR**, MINISTER OF PUBLIC ENTREPRISES AT THE TIME OF THE PROJECT, FOR HER PRESENCE AND SUPPORT AT THE PHOTOGRAPHERS' WELCOME DINNER, **DATO JAMES WONG**, MINISTER OF THE ENVIRONMENT AND TOURISM, SARAWAK, AND OFFICERS IN HIS MINISTRY ESPECIALLY DENIS HON, FOR THEIR ASSISTANCE AND HOSPITALITY IN KUCHING; **GENERAL TAN SRI HASHIM MOHD ALI**, CHIEF OF THE MALAYSIAN ARMED FORCES AND **LIEUTENANT-GENERAL DATO SERI HAJI MOHD YUNOS MOHD TASI**, CHIEF OF THE ROYAL MALAYSIAN AIR FORCE; THE HEADS OF THE RMAF BASES IN KUALA LUMPUR, BUTTERWORTH, KUCHING AND LABUAN AND THE RMAF PILOTS MAJ AMIN, MAJ ANNUAR, CPT BAKRI, B-G DATO FAUZI, MAJ LEE HOCK CHEW, LT MOHD YUSOF ISHAK, COL OII, COL RAHIM, MAJ ROSU AND MAJ SAMAON, WHO FLEW OUR PHOTOGRAPHERS IN THEIR HELICOPTERS. OUR HEARTFELT THANKS ALSO GO TO THE MEMBERS OF THE EDITORIAL ADVISORY BOARD, WHO BESIDES THEIR ADVISORY DUTIES ALSO CONTRIBUTED THE FOLLOWING ASSISTANCE: **TAN SRI DATO AZIZ ABDUL RAHMAN**, MANAGING DIRECTOR OF MALAYSIA AIRLINES, FOR HIS SUPPORT WHICH PROVIDED SMOOTH TRANSPORT ARRANGEMENTS FOR THE PROJECT; **TAN SRI ZAIN AZRAAI**, SECRETARY-GENERAL OF THE MINISTRY OF FINANCE, WHO CONTRIBUTED A LOT OF TIME, PERSONAL INSIGHT AND EXPERIENCE TO THE PRODUCTION OF THIS BOOK; **TAN SRI THONG YAW HONG**, CHAIRMAN OF SPORTS TOTO BERHAD, WHOSE ENTHUSIASM AND KEEN INTEREST HELPED KEEP THE SPIRITS OF THE PROJECT TEAM HIGH; **TAN SRI KISHU T JETHANAND**, CHAIRMAN OF GLOBE SILK STORE, FOR HIS ENTHUSIASTIC SUPPORT AND FOR THE PHOTOGRAPHERS' BATIK SHIRTS; **DATO AZIZ ISMAIL**, PRINCIPAL PRIVATE SECRETARY TO THE PRIME MINISTER, FOR HIS ASSISTANCE WITH THE NATIONAL DAY PARADE AND THE PRIME MINISTER'S LUNCH FOR THE PHOTOGRAPHERS AND SPONSORS; **PUAN AZAH AZIZ**, FOR HER GRACIOUS, EVER-SMILING AND KNOWLEDGEABLE SUPPORT; **ISMAIL ADAM**, DEPUTY SECRETARY-GENERAL OF THE MINISTRY OF CULTURE, ARTS AND TOURISM FOR HIS ASSISTANCE IN THE ARRANGEMENTS FOR THE PHOTOGRAPHERS' ASSIGNMENTS; **ISMAIL ZAIN**, ARTIST, AND HIS WIFE, WAIRAH MARZUKI, FOR THEIR TIME AND ENERGY IN BRIEFING THE PHOTOGRAPHERS AND WRITERS, AND **IBRAHIM HUSSEIN**, ARTIST, FOR HIS ENTHUSIASM, IDEAS AND ESPECIALLY FOR HIS SPECIAL CREATION IN COMMEMORATION OF THIS HISTORIC PROJECT. WE WOULD ALSO LIKE TO THANK THE FOLLOWING: IN **KUALA LUMPUR**: ALIA MOHAMMED JALLY, ARIFFIN JELANI, BADRI HAJI MASRI, BEN BOUSNINA, GUY CHAPLIN, MARIA DANKER, ANITA GORDON, HASNAH HAFEZ AHAMED, ALBERTO DEL HOYO, IBRAHIM KAMIL, THARAWAT ISMAIL BAKTI, IZAN YUSUFF, WAVENEY JENKINS, KADIR JASIN, KHALID AHMAD, N KRISHNAMOORTHY, KOH LEAN CHONG, LAT, DATO LIM KOK WING AND DATIN TESSIE LIM, ANDY LOW, ALICE LOW, MOKHZANI MAHATHIR, NARELLE MCMURTRIE, MOHD ALIAS KAUL, NADZMI MOHD SALLEH, DATO HAJI NIK IBRAHIM KAMIL, ERIC PERIS, RAMLI IBRAHIM, SHAHRIL SHAMSUDDIN, SHAMSUL BAHRI MD. TOKIT, TAN SRI DATO MUBIN SHEPPARD, SHUKOR KARIM, PC SHIVADAS, LIZ TAJUDDIN, ANGELA TAN, THAVEE CHOWRUNGRATANASARI, GERALD XAVIER AND ZAINURIN LAZIM. ON THE **EAST COAST**: RAJA BAHARIN SHAH, ROSELAN HANAFIAH, RAY HALL, TENGKU ISMAIL TENGKU SU, MOHD JUSOH, NIK ISMAIL CHE MUDA, SYED KAMARUZAMAN; **WEST COAST**: LINDA CH'NG, CHEAH LEE KHOOI, TUNKU IMRAN & TUNKU NAQUIYUDDIN IBNI TUANKU JAAFAR, KAMARUDDIN ZAKARIA, DR KHOO JOO EE, KEE PHAIK CHEEN, YAZAN AYUB, CHEN KIN CHOUN, NAZIR ARIFF, PANI, LIM SUAN HAR, LAURENCE LOH & MRS LOH, HAJI SYED AHMAD, DIANA TAN, KB TIONG AND DENNIS YONG. IN **EAST MALAYSIA**: PATRICK ANDAU, ADENAN SATEM, ELISABETH CHAN, RANDY DAVIS, EFFENDI NORWAWI, CAROLINE GOH, MAGDALENE GOH, HAJI GHAZALI, DAVID DE LA HARPE, PETER & LINDA IBOH, DATO JOSEPH JINGGUT, DR PETER KEDIT, ANTHONY LAMB, FRANCIS S P LIEW, RUTH LIM KONG, WOLFGANG MAIER, STANLEY MALANG, LINDA & TONY NGIMAT, MADELINE REGIS, ANDREW TAN, AND CATHY WANG. IN **SINGAPORE**: CHIU LENG CAMPOS, GINA MOK, WENDY GAN AND THE TIEN WAH PRESS PRODUCTION TEAM, JULIAN DAVISON, TAN EK BENG OF EKBEN GRAPHIC, JANICE TAN AND THE FA TEAM, TAN SOO BUAY AND HER SUPERSKILL GRAPHICS STAFF, HELEN WEST AND WOON MEE LAN. WE APOLOGISE IF WE HAVE INADVERTENTLY LEFT OUT ANYONE WHO HAS CONTRIBUTED TO THIS PROJECT.

BEAZLEY, A. Mitchell, *The Last Rainforests* (World Conservation Atlas, London, 1990)

BERNARD, Hans-Ulrich and BROOKE, Marcus, *Insight Guide: Wildlife of Southeast Asia* (APA, Hong Kong, 1991)

BIRD, Isabella, *The Golden Chersonese* (1883) (Oxford University Press, Kuala Lumpur, 1967)

BOCK, Carl, *The Head-hunters of Borneo* (1881) (OUP, Kuala Lumpur, 1985)

CAREY, Iskandar, *Orang Asli* (OUP, Kuala Lumpur, 1976)

CHIN, Lucas, *Cultural Heritage of Sarawak* (Sarawak Museum, Kuching, 1980)

CLIFFORD, Hugh Charles, *In Court and Kampung* (1897) (Graham Brash, Singapore, 1989)

GULLICK, J. M., *Kuala Lumpur 1880-1895* (1955) (Pelanduk, Kuala Lumpur, 1988)

GULLICK, J. M., *Malay Society in the Late 19th Century* (OUP, Kuala Lumpur, 1987)

HARRISSON, Tom, *World Within* (OUP, Singapore, 1959)

HONG, Evelyne, *Natives of Sarawak* (Institut Masyarakat, Penang, 1987)

HOSE, Charles, *Natural Man* (1926) (OUP, Kuala Lumpur, 1988)

HOSE, Charles, *The Field Book of a Jungle Wallah* (1929) (OUP, Kuala Lumpur, 1985)

HOSE, Charles and MCDOUGALL, William, *The Pagan Tribes of Borneo* (Macmillan, London, 1912)

Illustrated London News (selections)

KING, Ben, WOODCOCK, Martin & DICKENSON, E. C., *A Field Guide to the Birds of Southeast Asia* (Collins, London, 1975)

LAU, Dennis, *Penans: The Vanishing Nomads of Borneo* (Inter-State Publishing Co, Kota Kinabalu, 1987)

MACDONALD, Malcolm, *Borneo People* (Jonathan Cape, 1956)

MACKINNON, John, *In Search of the Red Ape* (Collins, London, 1974)

MCNEELY, Jeffrey A. and WACHTEL, Paul S., *Soul of the Tiger* (Doubleday, New York, 1988)

MEDWAY, Lord, *Mammals of Borneo* (Malaysian Branch of the Royal Asiatic Society, Kuala Lumpur, 1977)

MEDWAY, Lord, *The Wild Mammals of Malaya and Singapore* (OUP, Kuala Lumpur, 1978)

MORRISON, Hedda, *Sarawak* (Donald Moore Press Ltd, Singapore, 1965)

O'HANLON, Redmond, *Into the Heart of Borneo* (Penguin Books, London, 1984)

PAYNE, Junaidi, FRANCIS, Charles M. and PHILIPPS, Karen, *A Field Guide to the Mammals of Borneo* (The Sabah Society and WWF Malaysia, Kuala Lumpur, 1985)

PAYNE, Junaidi and CUBITT, Gerald, *Wild Malaysia* (New Holland, London, 1990)

RAWSON, Philip, *The Art of Southeast Asia* (Thames and Hudson, London, 1967)

RUBELI, Ken, *Tropical Rainforest in Southeast Asia* (Tropical Press, Kuala Lumpur, 1986)

SAVAGE, Victor R., *Western Impressions of Nature and Landscape in Southeast Asia* (Singapore University Press, Singapore, 1984)

SKEAT, Walter W., *Malay Magic* (1900) (OUP, 1984)

SMYTHIES, B. E., *The Birds of Borneo* (Oliver and Boyd, London, 1960)

TATE, D. J. M., *Rajah Brooke's Borneo* (Compiled by John Nicholson Ltd, Hong Kong, 1988)

WALLACE, Alfred Russell, *The Malay Archipelago* (1869) (Dover Publications Inc, New York, 1962)

Captions for opening pages: Sunset over Mt Kinabalu, *Page 1,* viewed from the Kinabalu National Park headquarters. The peaks of this mountain — the tallest in Southeast Asia — are nicknamed Donkey's Ears and Ugly Sister. *Pages 2-3:* Trengganu on the east coast of Peninsular Malaysia has fishing villages with their atap huts, sampans and fishing boats, over which the sun rises in a spectacular way most mornings. *Page 6:* Langkawi, off the northwest coast of Peninsular Malaysia, is an island of legends in an archipelago of 104 isles famous for their white beaches and clear waters. *Pages 8-9:* In the Bareo Highlands of Sarawak in East Malaysia, the Kelabit tribe plant hill padi in irrigated fields. *Pages 10-11:* Sunrise over the Sultan Salahuddin Abdul Aziz Mosque in Shah Alam, Selangor. *Page 12:* The majestic songket, made of heavy gold-thread brocade, is the traditional attire of the sultans.